COFFEE

COFFEE

A Guide to Buying, Brewing and Enjoying

Revised Edition

KENNETH DAVIDS

Illustrations by M. L. Duniec

101 Productions

Library of Congress Catalog Card Number 88-71981
ISBN 0-89721-163-4

CONTENTS

INTRODUCING IT
The information gap; the perfect cup; specialty vs. commercial coffees

WHEN I PRODUCED the first edition of this book in the mid-1970s, finding a bag of freshly roasted specialty coffee was an act of esoteric consumerism often requiring miles of freeway travel and journeys into select corners of certain large American cities. And if you wanted a decent cappuccino, you were in even bigger trouble; you might have to trek halfway across town (or halfway across the country).

Today the yuppie phenomenon, for all of its kiwi-slicing and homemade-purple-pasta affectation, has brought with it a genuine culinary revolution in the United States. And with it, a specialty coffee store (it seems) on every gentrified urban street corner and a cappuccino machine in every restaurant. Furthermore, the latest culinary transformation clearly has sunk deeper than fad and affectation; it has reached even our palates, our sensual being. I find nearly everywhere in my travels around America decent cappuccini where there used to be nothing but whipped-cream pretensions, or waitresses dangling Silex carafes.

To give you a statistic: When I sold my café in Berkeley, it was one of about five or six such establishments in the entire town, and one of

INTRODUCING IT

three putting out a decent cappuccino. Today a newspaper article tells me there are 30 cafés on one side of the University of California campus alone, selling close to 40,000 cups of Italian coffee a day, or 1.2 cups per day, per student, not excluding tea drinkers and puritans.

Blue Mountain syndrome

If the current Europeanizing of American habits is based on the genuine sensual perception of quality, such was not the case even a few years ago. At that time I kept running across the Jamaican Blue Mountain syndrome: well-meaning middle-class families, with no idea what really fine coffee tasted like, buying fancy coffee at $18 a pound to impress their guests and storing it in their refrigerator for two months, where it went terminally rancid. I also ran across small specialty roasters changing hands and going big time, in the process replacing attention to quality with attention to marketing, and even slipping into shoddy habits like reroasting returned coffees or spraying perfectly decent coffee with oils and flavorings.

better-educated consumers

Today, five years later, there appears to be something of a counter-reaction. Better-educated consumers have led to more responsible retailing practices in the specialty-coffee industry. If there is a falloff in quality today, it is probably happening at the level of the coffee producer and distributor. If you are a grower with a famous coffee on your hands—with Japanese, North Americans, and Germans all bidding for it—you may naturally want to produce more of that coffee; more than is commensurate with maintaining the quality that made it famous in the first place. Or, if you are a wholesaler facing the same demand, you may begin to make discreet substitutes: for instance, lower-priced Ethiopian coffees mixed in with the somewhat similar, but higher-priced Yemen Mocha coffees.

a sensual experience

Nevertheless, the implicit theme of this book is well on its way to prevailing: Coffee is a sensual experience as well as a wake-up pill, and if it is drunk at all it should be drunk well and deliberately; drunk as we drink good wine, rather than swilled half cold out of Styrofoam while we work. And I say terrific; maybe enjoying good coffee won't save the world, but it certainly won't hurt.

There still appears to be something of a knowledge gap, however, a space between consumer aspiration and fulfillment. More and more consumers may know where they're going, but many may still need a little help getting there. This attitude became most clear to me when I was in a large store in Berkeley researching prices on the latest espresso machines. Five years ago there would have been two or three machines on display and passers-by would have asked me what you did with them. Now there were 20 machines on display and I was asked a series of very detailed technical questions by a group of rather well-informed consumers. Their questions revealed that this cross-section of Northern California department-store-browsers knew very well what a good cappuccino should taste like, but were uncertain about what steps to take to produce one at home: They wanted advice on details: about which machine to choose, about frothing milk, and about choosing and grinding espresso coffees. They knew, in other words, what they wanted, but simply needed a little advice about how to achieve it. The same might be said for visitors to specialty coffee stores: Customers are convinced, for instance, that freshly roasted, whole-bean coffees taste better than canned, but still seem tentative on details.

advice on details

This book is addressed to that gap between coffee aspiration and fulfillment, as well as to any casual, nonconverted readers who may doubt that coffee offers a world of pleasure and connoisseurship as rich and interesting as wine, and well worth the same attention. It is not another gift cookbook filled with foreign exclamations and inedible recipes stolen from other cookbooks, recipes that you try once, during the week between Christmas and New Year's. It *is* a practical book about a small but real pleasure, with real advice about how to buy better coffee, make better coffee, enjoy coffee in more ways, avoid destroying yourself with caffeine while drinking coffee, and, if you care to, talk about coffee with authority. Throughout, I've tried to blend the practical and experimental with the historical and descriptive, and produce a book simultaneously useful in the kitchen and entertaining in the armchair.

a practical book

INTRODUCING IT

The present relatively high price of coffee is one more reason to approach the drink with love and respect. Coffee is high priced only when compared to cheap tea. A cup of the world's finest coffee, for instance, costs less than the same amount of Coca-Cola and is 10 to 15 times cheaper than a wine of similar distinction.

the perfect cup I used to stay at a little run-down hotel in Ensenada, Mexico, overlooking the harbor. The guests gathered every morning in a big room filled with threadbare carpets and magazine chromos of the Swiss Alps, to sit on broken-down couches, sip the hotel coffee, and look out at the harbor through some sagging French doors.

Nachita, the old woman who ran the hotel, made the coffee herself, from very cheap, black-roasted, sugar-glazed beans. I assume the beans were

Box Grinder

the carelessly picked and primitively processed type called "naturals" in the coffee trade, because the coffee had a certain rank bitterness associated with such beans, a taste which is never forgotten. Nachita's tendency to lightly boil the coffee didn't help much either. At any rate, by the time the coffee got to us it was dark, muddy, and sourly bitter, with a persistence no amount of sugar could overcome nor Carnation evaporated milk obscure.

By anyone's standards it was bad coffee. But—you can guess the rest—the morning, the sun on the sea, the chickens in the back yard, the mildewed smell of Nachita's carpets and the damp smell of old stone walls, the clumsy bilingual conversations, the glorious poems about mornings and Mexico I never put on paper, got mixed up with that sour bitterness and turned it into something more than perfect; I loved it. I even loved the tinny sweetness of the condensed milk. After all, there wasn't any other cup of coffee, and I was happy.

A cup of coffee is as much a moment caught in the matrix of time and space as it is a beverage; "perfect" cup of coffee to whom and when?

Of course there are certain universals in good coffee making, which run through this book like comforting refrains: good water, good beans properly *certain universals* roasted and freshly ground, careful brewing, and so on, all of which fortunately do not depend on sleazily exotic mornings in Ensenada, and work even at five o'clock on rainy Sundays in Cleveland.

There is plentiful indication, for instance, that the steady decline in coffee drinking in the United States (the near three cups a day the average American drank 20 years ago has now shrunk to fewer than two cups) is owing to the widespread use of instant coffees which lack both flavor and aroma. Why else would the consumption of quality coffees be increasing spectacularly, while the consumption of commercial coffees continues to decrease?

Nevertheless, the consumer of the average tasteless, thin-bodied instant may be in for a bit of a surprise when he tastes his first cup of one of the

ARABIAN COFFEE ROASTING

world's great, rich, full-bodied coffees. If one gets used to living in a studio apartment, a mansion may feel a little uncomfortable—for the first week.

Furthermore, the best cup of Middle Eastern–style coffee, say, will taste like a cross between cough syrup and ice-cream topping to an American, while the Middle Easterner would probably use the contents of the American's Chemex to polish the buckles on his camel harness (or the bumper on his European automobile). Even with good coffee, tastes differ.

Coffee drinkers worldwide can be divided by habit and preference into three great traditions: first, the Middle East; second, southern Europe and Latin America; and third, North Americans, northern Europeans, and the rest of the pale-faced, English-speaking world.

three great traditions

Middle Easterners remain closest to basics. They like their coffee roasted dark, generally; grind it to a powder, generally; bring their coffee to a boil several times, always; and produce a small, bittersweet cup heavy with sugar and sediment. The little cups are sipped with a ceremonious air, at all times of the day, and nobody rushes.

The southern European or city-dwelling Latin American has two perfect cups, one for morning and one for afternoon and evening. He always prefers his coffee dark roasted, bitter, almost burned. He usually prefers it from an espresso machine, a big machine that dribbles out small amounts of strong, black, heavy-bodied brew, foamy on top, with a little, not a lot, of sediment in the cup. In the morning he mixes a stiff shot of this stuff with hot milk in a big bowl or tall, wide-mouthed glass, something he can really get his hands around. He wants to warm his palms and fill his nostrils with it, dip his roll in it; if he could, he'd probably take a bath in it. At night or in the afternoon, however, the southern European's perfect cup is as small as the Middle Easterner's, maybe one-fourth the size of his morning bowl, black, but just as strong and sweet.

palm-warming and nostril-filling

The perfect cup of English-speaking coffee is at the furthest remove from the Middle Easterner's. First, beans roasted brown, not black, without a trace of the burned, bitter tang of Europe or the Middle East. The beverage

INTRODUCING IT

must be clear (*no* sediment!), light, smooth, and so delicate milk or even sugar tends to overwhelm any pretense to body or flavor.

The typical North American neither immerses himself in big bowls every morning, nor saves his coffee for after dinner, nor takes quick little sips out of tiny cups with ceremonial deliberation. He drinks the stuff all day out of office urns, or carries a half-filled cup around while doing the housework. And as has often been pointed out, the North American's coffee is his beverage as well as his dessert; he not only finishes meals with it, he's liable to start and middle with it, too.

a fourth tradition   Finally, there is a fourth tradition which is dangerously close to swamping all the other three: dumping a spoonful of brown powder in a Styrofoam cup of hot water and drinking it while walking out the door into the smog. This tradition has of late become well established in all parts of the world. A friend reports that she was unable to find anything except Nescafé in the cafés of Guatemala Antigua, the home of one of the world's finest coffees. The final blow, however, came in Guadalajara, where she ordered a cappuccino and watched in stunned silence as the counterman turned from the gleaming espresso machine to dump a spoonful of brown powder into a cup of foamed milk.

One reason for such a paradox, of course, is the fact that the best Mexican and Central American coffee is bought by the United States whereas the locals can only afford the cheapest grades of local coffee, and may prefer a decent instant instead. But I can't help but feel the reasons are more than economic; I'm sure instant coffee is part of the whole anti-sensual, compulsive work ethic of industrialism, creeping over the world like the shadow of a giant billboard. After all, instant makes for considerably shorter coffee breaks.

At any rate, readers of this book need not feel limited by any tradition. A cup of coffee like any other gesture can be enriched by choice and consciousness. The pages following offer you not the "perfect cup," but the perfect *cups*.

All the coffees I will be advising you to buy are known in the trade as "specialty" coffees. The opposite of specialty is "commercial" coffee. From the consuming end the most immediately noticeable difference between commercial and specialty coffees is packaging: Commercial coffee comes in little bottles of instant, or already ground and packed in a tin. Specialty coffee comes as whole beans, in either one-pound bags or in bulk, and needs to be ground before it's brewed.

Commercial coffee is usually roasted and packed in large plants, under nationally advertised brand names; specialty coffee is usually roasted in small stores or factories, using traditional methods and technology, and is often sold where it's roasted.

Specialty coffees offer considerably more choice than commercial coffees; you can buy coffee by the place the bean originated ("Kenya," "Colombian"); by roast ("French roast," "Italian roast "); or by blend designed for the time of day, price or flavor. Commercial coffees offer only a very limited selection of blend and roast, and little possibility whatsoever of buying straight, unblended coffees.

Specialty coffees offer more opportunity for the consumer to participate in the creation of his pleasure; commercial coffees are a *fait accompli* in a tin or bag.

The final, most important difference between commercial and specialty coffees is the way they taste and smell. The best commercial blended coffees are good. The worst are atrocious. But bought fresh and brewed correctly, specialty coffees are more than good; they are superb, and superb in a variety of ways. If you want to know how specialty coffees get to be better than commercial coffees, read on. If you take my word for it, skip to Chapter 2.

Coffee buyers divide the world's coffee production into three main categories: "high-grown mild," "Brazilian," and "robusta."

High-grown mild coffees demand the highest prices on the world

SPECIALTY VS.
COMMERCIAL

WHY BUY SPECIALTY

INTRODUCING IT

market. The coffee tree will not tolerate frost, but will not flourish when temperatures are extremely high either. This means coffee grows best in certain well-watered, mountainous regions of the tropics. High-grown mild

high-grown mild

coffees, no matter where they come from, are grown at altitudes over 2,000 feet above sea level, usually between 4,000 and 6,000 feet. They are also produced from berries that are picked only when ripe, and prepared with care. The responsible specialty coffee roaster uses only the finest high-grown mild coffees.

"Brazilian"

The use of the term "Brazilian" to describe the next most preferred group of coffees is misleading, since Brazil also produces excellent mild coffees. The trade term "Brazilian," however, refers to lower-grade coffees which are grown at low altitudes on vast plantations and mass harvested. These coffees at best have a middle-of-the-road, neutral flavor, with a flat aroma. Most decent commercial blends contain large proportions of "Brazilian," with smaller additions of high-grown milds.

Both "high-grown mild" and "Brazilian" coffees are produced from plants which belong to the botanical species *Coffea arabica.* The arabica is the original coffee plant; it still grows wild in Ethiopia, and was first cultivated in Yemen at the southern tip of the Arabian peninsula. *Coffea arabica* was then carried around the world by coffee-hooked devotées, much as European wine grapes spread to form the basis of the world's wine industry. All specialty coffees come from *Coffea arabica* stock, which still makes up the majority of the world's production.

robusta

Many other species of coffee tree grow wild in Africa, however, and one, the *Coffea robusta*, has grown to major importance in world markets. The main advantages of the robusta are its resistance to disease, and the fact that it will grow successfully at lower altitudes than *Coffea arabica.* The bean, however, does not have the fragrance or flavor of the best arabica, or even a decent Brazilian, and demands the lowest prices in the world market. Robusta is used as a component in the cheapest American commercial coffees, especially instant coffees.

The coffee bean, like all beans, is a seed; it grows at the heart of a small berry, about the size of the end of your little finger. Before the coffee can be shipped and roasted the bean must be separated from the berry. Nature has been particularly lavish in its protection of the coffee bean, and removing the three sets of skin and one layer of pulp from around the bean is a complex process. If done properly, the coffee looks better, tastes better and demands a higher price.

The worst preparation would be as follows: The coffee berries are stripped—leaves, unripe berries, and all—onto the ground. This mixture is then scooped up, sifted, dried in big piles, and some time later the hardened berry is stripped off the bean. Some beans will be small and deformed, shriveled, or discolored. In poorly prepared coffee all the beans, good and bad, plus a few twigs, a little dirt, and some stones, are shipped together. The various flavor taints associated with cheap coffee—earthiness, mustiness, harshness, and so on—derive from careless picking and drying.

the worst preparation

The best preparation would run like this: The beans are selectively picked as they ripen. The outer skin is immediately scraped loose, exposing the pulp. The beans are then soaked, and the sweet pulp fermented off the bean. More soaking, or more properly washing, follows, before the bean is dried and the last layers of skin, now dry and crumbly, are stripped off the bean. In some cases, the beans are further tumbled and "polished" to improve their appearance.

the best

Coffee is graded according to these three criteria: the quality of the bean (altitude and species), quality of preparation, and size of the bean. A fourth criterion is simply how good the coffee tastes and smells, what coffee people call "cup quality."

Again: The specialty coffee seller buys only the best grades of coffee, which means high-grown mild beans, excellent preparation, with high cup quality. When you buy from a responsible specialty coffee seller you should be buying top quality, no matter what country of origin or roast you choose.

KALDI & the DANCING GOATS

1 HOW IT STARTED
The odyssey of the bean

THE MOST FAMOUS version of the origin of coffee goes like this: Once upon a time in the land of Arabia Felix, lived a goatherd named Kaldi. Kaldi was a sober, responsible goatherd, whose goats were also sober, if not responsible. One night Kaldi's goats didn't come home, and in the morning he found them dancing in abandoned glee near a shiny, dark-leaved shrub with red berries. Kaldi soon determined that it was the red berries on the shiny, dark-leaved shrub that caused their eccentric behavior, and it wasn't long before he was dancing, too.

Finally a learned *innam* from a local monastery came by, sleepily, no doubt, on his way to prayer. He saw the goats dancing, Kaldi dancing, and the shiny, dark-leaved shrub with the red berries. Being of a more systematic turn of mind than the goats or Kaldi, the learned *innam* subjected the red berries to various experimental examinations, one of which involved parching and boiling. Soon neither the *innam* nor his fellows fell asleep at prayers, and the use of coffee spread from monastery to monastery, throughout Arabia Felix, and from there to the world. We never find out whether Kaldi and his goats dropped dead from exhaustion and caffeine poisoning, or learned to control their habit.

a sleepy monk

15

HOW IT STARTED

Owing to stories like this, coffee was first thought to have originated in what is now Yemen, on the Arabian peninsula, where Europeans first found it growing. But botanical evidence indicates *Coffea arabica* originated

Ethiopia on the plateaus of central Ethiopia, several thousand feet above sea level, where it still grows wild, shaded by the enormous umbrella-like trees of the rain forest. How it got from Ethiopia to Yemen is uncertain. One guess is those "Arabian traders" who always seem to be schlepping things around in history books. Another possibility is the Persians, who during their leisurely invasions of Egypt and Yemen around the sixth century A.D. could have brought coffee with them from Ethiopia across the Red Sea to Yemen. At any rate, *Coffea arabica* seems to have been cultivated in Yemen from about the sixth century on. Black African cultures used coffee earlier, but as a solid food, combined with animal fat, for instance, or chewed like nuts.

In Arabia coffee was first mentioned as a medicine, then as a beverage
coffee takes taken in connection with meditation and religious exercises by dervishes.
to the streets From there it moved into the streets and virtually created a new institution, the coffee house. Once visitors from the rest of the world tasted it in the coffee houses of Cairo and Mecca, the spread of *Coffea arabica* was, by 16th-century standards, electrifyingly rapid. The extraordinary story of the dissemination of *Coffea arabica* from the seed of possibly *one tree* to virtually the entire world is full of the sort of passion and sacrifice that must come from deeper springs than greed alone. Everywhere that people tasted coffee they wanted it, and went through extraordinary pains to bring some home with them.

The arabica plant's amazing odyssey was only possible because of its stubborn botanical self-reliance; it pollinates itself, which means mutations are much less likely to occur than in plants which have a light pollen and require cross-fertilization. Most differences in flavor between arabica beans are caused not so much by differences in the plants themselves, but by the subtle variations wrought by soil, moisture, and climate. The plant itself has remained extraordinarily true to itself through five centuries of plantings around the world.

At first the Arabs, jealous of their discovery, refused to allow fertile seed to leave their country, insisting that all beans be first parched or boiled. *the seven seeds* All this jealous care was doomed to obvious failure, however, and it was inevitable that someone, in this case a Moslem pilgrim from India named Baba Budan, should sneak some seeds out of Arabia. Legend says he bound "seven seeds" to his belly, and as soon as he reached his home hermitage, a cave in the hills near Chikamalagur in south India, he planted them and they flourished. In 1928, William Ukers reported in his encyclopedic work *All About Coffee* that the descendants of these first seeds "still grow beneath gigantic jungle trees near Chikamalagur," presumably keeping other hermits alert and praising Allah.

From the descendents of the "seven seeds" coffee plants spread up and down mainland India. The French became interested, but their attempt to propagate coffee in southern France, near Dijon, failed because the tree does not tolerate frost. The more enterprising Dutch, however, carried plants from Malabar, in India, the descendents of the first "seven seeds" of Baba Budan, on to Java, where after some effort coffee growing was established on a regular basis.

It was at this point in our history that coffee made its debut as the everyday pleasure of noblemen and other Europeans rich enough to afford exotic luxuries. Coffee was available either from Mocha, the main port of Yemen, or from Java. Hence the famous blend of "Mocha-Java," which in those days meant putting together in one drink the entire possible world of coffee experience.

Now comes one of the most extraordinary stories in the spread of coffee, the "saga of the noble tree." Louis XIV of France, with his insatiable *the noble tree* curiosity and love of luxury, was of course by this time an ardent coffee drinker. The Dutch owed him a favor, and managed, with great difficulty, to procure him a coffee tree. The tree had originally been obtained at the

Arabian port of Mocha, then carried to Java, and then, finally, back across the seas to Holland, where it was brought overland to Paris. As soon as Louis saw that tree his eyes lit up. He is said to have spent an entire day communing with it himself, before turning it over to his botanists. The first greenhouse in Europe was constructed to house the noble tree: it flowered, bore fruit, and became one of the most prolific parents in the history of plantdom.

This was in 1715. From that single tree, billions of arabica trees, including most presently growing in Central and South America, sprung. However, true to the kinky karma of coffee, the odyssey of the offspring of the noble tree was not easy or straightforward.

The first sprouts from the noble tree reached Martinique in the Caribbean in about 1720, owing to the truly heroic efforts of Chevalier Gabriel Mathiew de Clieu, who assuredly follows Baba Budan into the coffee hall of fame. De Clieu first had difficulties talking the authorities in Paris into giving him some trees (he finally stole them), but this was nothing to what he went

a coffee saboteur

through once at sea. First, a fellow traveler tried to rip up his trees, a man who, De Clieu writes, was "basely jealous of the joy I was about to taste through being of service to my country, and being unable to get this coffee plant away from me, tore off a branch." Other, more cynical commentators suggest the potential coffee thief was a Dutch spy bent on sabotaging the French coffee industry.

Later, the ship barely eluded some pirates, nearly sunk in a storm, and was finally becalmed. Water grew scarce, and all but one of the precious little seedlings died. Now comes the most poignant episode of all: De Clieu, though suffering from thirst himself, was so desperately looking forward to coffee in the New World that he shared half of his daily water ration with his struggling charge, "upon which," he writes, "my happiest hopes were founded. . . . It needed such succor the more in that it was extremely backward, being no larger than the slip of a pink."

Once this spindly shoot of the noble tree reached Martinique, however, it flourished; 50 years later there were 18,791,680 coffee trees in Martinique, and coffee cultivation was established in Haiti, Mexico, and most of the islands of the Caribbean.

De Clieu became one of coffee's greatest heroes, honored in song and story. Pardon, in *La Martinique,* says he deserves a place in history next to Parmentier, who brought the potato to France. Esmenard, a writer of navigational epics, exclaims:

> With that refreshing draught his life he will not cheer;
> But drop by drop revives the plant he holds more dear.
> Already as in dreams, he sees great branches grow,
> One look at his dear plant assuages all his woe.

The noble tree also sent shoots to the island of Réunion, in the Indian Ocean, then called the Isle of Bourbon. This plant was found to be a somewhat different variety of arabica, with smaller beans, and was named *var. bourbon.* The famed Santos coffees of Brazil and the Oaxaca coffees of Mexico are said to be the offspring of the Bourbon tree, which by now had traveled from Ethiopia to Mocha, from Mocha to Java, from Java to a hot house in Holland, from there to Paris, from there to Réunion and eventually back halfway around the world to Brazil and Mexico. For the final irony, we have to wait until 1893, when coffee seed from Brazil was introduced into Kenya and Tanganyika, only a few hundred miles south of its original home in Ethiopia, thus completing a six-century circumnavigation of the globe.

variety Bourbon

Finally, to round out our set of coffee notables, we add the Don Juan of coffee propagation, Francisco de Melho Palheta of Brazil. The emperor of Brazil was interested in cutting his country into the coffee market, and in about 1727 sent De Melho Palheta to French Guiana, to obtain seeds. Like the Arabs and the Dutch before them, the French were jealously guarding their treasure, and Don Francisco, whom legend pictures as suave and deadly charming, had a hard time getting at those seeds. Fortunately for coffee drinkers, Don Francisco so successfully charmed the French Governor's wife that she sent him, buried in a bouquet of flowers, all the seeds and shoots he needed to initiate Brazil's billion-dollar coffee industry.

the Don Juan of coffee growing

2 BUYING IT
What the names mean; choosing coffee by roast

T HE FIRST DECISION in drinking coffee is where to buy it. There are roughly four strategies for purchasing specialty coffees: First, you can order by mail, which is at best an expedient and should only be indulged in if there are no specialty coffee suppliers in your town. Second, you can buy from a supermarket with a selection of whole-bean coffees and a do-it-yourself grinder. Third, you can buy from a "gourmet" food market or the fancy foods section of a large department store. Fourth, you can buy from a specialty coffee store.

The price may be lowest at the supermarket for all the well-advertised reasons: lower markup, brisker competition, higher volume. The same coffee at a specialty coffee store may cost up to 10 percent more, but you have many advantages: You can buy less than a pound at a time (a big advantage if you don't grind your own), request special blends, impress the clerk with your knowledge of coffee, sample new coffees, and wander around staring at the little machines and gadgets. As for the third alternative, the gourmet food market or department store, whole-bean coffees found in such places are often excellent, but if sales volume is low and the manager disinterested, you may find yourself buying a stale coffee held too

where to buy

long on the shelf. Most stores specializing only in coffee, or in coffee and tea, care too much about their product to sell it less than fresh.

Your next problem may be finding a specialty coffee store, or choosing among them. With kitchen fundamentalists, new-wave gourmets, and economy-class jet-age cosmopolitans transforming our food-shopping habits, most good-sized North American cities now have dozens of specialty coffee and tea sellers. You can find them listed in the yellow pages under "Coffee Sellers Retail." If there are none, you could call supermarkets to see whether they handle whole-bean coffees, or check the back of this book for mail-order addresses. If you are isolated from convenient sources for coffee, and you really enjoy it, you should definitely consider roasting your own, an enjoyable and surprisingly simple procedure; see Chapter 4.

Specialty coffee stores usually fall into one of the following categories:

- Roast their own coffee on the premises or nearby.
- As part of a chain, roast their own coffee at a central location.
- Buy their coffee from another local specialty roaster.
- Buy their coffee from several roasters.
- Buy their coffee green and have it roasted for them.

more exciting To me stores falling into the first category are most exciting, and I suggest that in general you buy your coffee as close to the person who does the roasting as possible. The coffee will be fresher, often better, and the salesperson more informed.

And then, of course, you can visit shops and taste their coffee. Some specialty coffee stores, peculiar though it may sound, brew their coffee badly, so it's hard to tell anything about their beans from their samples. On the other hand, many specialty stores will brew *fresh* samples of their coffees to order for potential customers. The most common solution is to keep two coffees brewing at a time, and to rotate the choices.

If no roasting machinery is in evidence, you might ask where the shop obtains its coffee. Half—maybe all—the stores in your area may get their coffee from the same roaster. A prominent San Francisco specialty roaster, for instance, sells his excellent coffee to supermarkets and specialty stores all over the San Francisco Bay Area, but his name seldom appears on the bag. *from the same roaster*

Of course even two shops that buy from the same supplier may differ in their handling of coffees. Staling begins the moment a coffee leaves the roasting machine, and a coffee sold by one shop a week after roasting will be significantly better than the same coffee sold elsewhere after three weeks. Look for well-established shops, large volume, and a proprietor who cares.

In cities with large European neighborhoods, one occasionally finds stores or cafés where a few (sometimes only one) fine coffees are roasted and sold as they were before the victory of convenience foods and canned coffees. These places often produce the best in their line, though for a wide range of coffees and equipment you must go elsewhere.

Many stores carry as many as 30 varieties of coffee. Each one has a name, plus a few aliases. Take heart, however. No matter how many names there are, they all refer to either the degree to which the bean is roasted, the place the bean came from *before* it was roasted, or the dealer's name for a blend of beans. ALL THOSE NAMES

Now look at the samples in the cases. You will notice that some are darker in color than others. You should also note that most names given these darker coffees are European, i.e., French, Italian, Viennese, continental, etc. These coffees are distinguished by the *length of time the bean is roasted*. Italian roast, for instance, is usually darker and has been roasted longer than Viennese. These names *do not* refer to the origin of the beans, however. Sometimes specialty coffee sellers specify the coffee which they have chosen to dark roast; in this case the coffee will be given a double-decked label like "Dark Roast Colombian" or "Italian Roasted Mexican." In most cases, however, the coffee a roaster chooses for his darker roasts will be an inexpensive blend of coffees from a variety of countries, and the name will refer only to the roast, not to the origin of the bean. *European names*

Next to the coffees with European names, which will differ in color, you will note coffees which show the same light-to-medium brown color, and carry exotic, non-European names, like Sumatran, Kenya, or Mexican. Unlike the coffees with European names, these coffees are roasted about the same length of time, or to what the roaster considers typical "American" tastes. The difference here is not the roast, but *the origin of the bean itself.* A coffee labeled Sumatran, for instance, will consist entirely of beans from a single crop in a single country, Sumatra. Since coffee can only be grown successfully in or very near the tropics, such straight varietal coffees tend to carry names of an exotic and sultry timbre.

Straight coffees, in addition to the name of the country in which they originated, often carry qualifying names: "Guatemalan Antigua," "Kenya AA," "Java Arabica," "Colombia Plantation," and so on. Most of these qualifying terms are either grade designations ("AA"), or market names referring to coffee-growing regions ("Antigua"). A few, like "Arabica," describe a botanical species or variety, and epithets like "Plantation" or "Estate" indicate coffee grown on a large farm rather than peasant plots.

market names

I discuss market names at length in Chapter 3, under the countries to which they refer. There are literally thousands in the coffee trade, but fortunately only the most famous find their way into the vocabulary of the specialty coffee retailer. Some derive from the name of a district, province, or state; others from a mountain range or similar landmark; others from a nearby important city; and still others from the name of a port or shipping point. Oaxaca coffees from Mexico are named for the state of Oaxaca; the Kilimanjaro coffees of Tanzania for the slopes of the mountain on which these coffees are grown. The Harrar coffees of Ethiopia take their name from the old city of Harrar; the Santos coffees of Brazil from the name of the port through which they are shipped.

grade names

Retailers may also qualify coffee labels by grade name. Grading, of course, is a device for controlling the quality of an agricultural commodity so that buyer and seller can do business without personally examining every lot sold. Coffee-grading terminology is unfortunately varied and obscure:

every coffee-growing country has its own set of terms, and few are distinguished by their logical clarity. "Kenya AA" is an exception: Clearly "AA" is better than "A" or "B." But though the Colombian terms "excelso" and "supremo" are both clearly laudatory, one could hardly determine by the terms alone that "supremo" is the single highest grade of Colombian coffee, and "excelso" a more comprehensive grade consisting of a mixture of supremo and the less desirable "extra" grade. And although one may be aware that altitude is a prime grading factor in Central American coffees, one could hardly guess without coaching that "strictly hard bean" refers to Guatemalan coffees grown on plantations situated at altitudes of 4,500 to 5,000 feet, and "hard bean" 4,000 to 4,500 feet. The higher the altitude the slower maturing the bean, and the harder and denser its substance, hence "hard bean."

The average specialty coffee retailer's use of terminology in labeling his coffees is seldom logical or even consistent, even when dealing with straight coffees. Ideally one ought to be made aware of the country and region where the coffee originated, its grade, its botanical variety if relevant, and even the market name of the plantation or co-operative where it was grown or processed. The month and year it was harvested would also be helpful. But the retailer usually tacks, at most, one qualifying adjective onto the name of the country of origin and lets it go at that. Some retailers may choose the most significant qualifying adjective, others the most romantic, but the end result *most romantic* is still confusion. The reader who manages Chapter 3 should also manage the terminology fairly well, however, and at least be in a position to make intelligent deductions.

To find out how capable you are at this point of surmounting such confusion, try this: *Kenya.* A tropical name, therefore a straight coffee from Kenya, roasted medium brown to American tastes. *Kenya AA.* The qualifying adjective, AA, doesn't sound like a place, and has a superlative *a test* ring to it, so you figure it must be a grade. Of course, you're correct. *Sumatran Mandheling.* A tropical name, therefore a straight coffee from

BUYING IT

Sumatra roasted medium brown; since Mandheling doesn't sound like a grade nor have you heard it mentioned as a botanical variety, you assume it is a market name referring to a specific coffee-growing region in Sumatra. You have deduced correctly. *Mexican Altura Coatepec.* Another straight coffee roasted medium brown, from Mexico. Coatepec sounds like a regional name; Altura has that superlative ring we associate with grades, and if you're at all familiar with Spanish you'll know it means heights, so you assume it's the name of a grade based on the altitude at which the coffee is grown. Correct. *French.* They don't grow coffee in France, so it must be a roast, darker than usual. Pick any prize on the lower shelf. *French-roast Mexican Oaxaca Pluma.* First of all a straight coffee from Mexico roasted more darkly than usual. Since Oaxaca is a city in Mexico, you figure (correctly) that Oaxaca refers to the region in Mexico where the coffee was grown. That leaves Pluma, which must be either a botanical variety or a grade; you guess grade and you're right. Any prize on the top shelf, including the pandas.

Deduction is even more in order when one begins to deal with blended coffees. Blends, of course, are mixtures of two or more straight coffees. *blended* There are two reasons to blend beans: one is to make a coffee with a flavor *coffees* that is either better and more complete, or at least different from the flavor produced by a straight coffee. The other is to cut costs while producing a palatable drink.

Nearly all commercial coffee sold in cans or bags is blended. Commercial roasters might want to market a Sumatran, for instance, but they can't be sure enough of an adequate supply of the same coffee month after month to warrant the expense in getting a name accepted by the public.

With many blends found in specialty coffee shops the name gives us some clue as to the origin of the coffees involved. The simplest to interpret is the famous mixture of one-third Yemen Mocha and two-thirds Java Arabica, the "Mocha-Java" of tradition. Such a blend is not designed to save money, but rather to blend two coffees that complement one another: Yemen Mocha is a sharp, distinctive, medium-bodied coffee, whereas Java is smoother, deeper-toned, and richer. Together the two coffees make a more complete beverage than either one on its own.

Other blends are named after the dominant straight coffee and combine a cheaper neutrally flavored coffee with a more expensive "name" coffee. Thus we have "Jamaica Mountain Blend," or "Mocha Blend." The characteristics of the name coffee will still come through, less intensely than in a straight coffee, but distinctive enough if the blending is done right, and at a savings to the consumer. In other cases, the blender may use lesser-known coffees to mimic the characteristics of a more famous and hard-to-get or expensive coffee; thus we have "Jamaica *Style*" coffee, or "Kona *Style* Blend."

Another tendency in blend nomenclature might be called the generally geographical. We find a "Central American Blend," or a "Caribbean Blend." Or we meet blends named for the time of day we presumably might drink them: "Breakfast Blend" usually means a blend of brisk, lighter-bodied coffees roasted more lightly than "After-Dinner Blends," which are usually made up of heavier-bodied coffees carried to a darker roast.

generally geographical

At this point we reach the ultimate test: the mysteriously named house blends, the beloved children of the proprietor or roaster, baptized with names of his personal fantasy. A specialty roaster may have one such child or a dozen. Some of these offspring may have been a tradition in a coffee-roasting family for a couple of generations; others may have been born yesterday; a few may be in detail at least unique; but most are standard blends well known in the coffee business, with slightly different proportions and fanciful names. Occasionally the name gives us a clue as to content, but most often we're faced with the arbitrary romance of the proprietor, whose preferences may run from mountaineering ("Tip of the Andes Blend"), to the elegantly British ("Mayfair"), to the darkly Latin ("Orsi").

I confess to mixed feelings about all vaguely named blends. Romance and imagination are marvelous qualities and should be encouraged, but I also think the consumer deserves to be informed in a direct and unpatronizing

mixed feelings

way. I would prefer a little explicit description along with the imagination, just a line or two about origins and proportions. But for now, one can only ask questions and taste, which is excellent advice anyhow, regardless of how explicit the label.

*particularly
ambiguous*

A last few terms that are particularly ambiguous: "Turkish" coffee refers neither to coffee from Turkey nor roast: The name designates *grind* of coffee and *style* of brewing. "Turkish" is a common name for a medium- to dark-roasted coffee, ground to a powder, sweetened, boiled and served with the sediment still in the cup. "Viennese" is a slippery one. It can mean a somewhat darker-than-normal roast, or a *blend* of *roasts* (about half dark and half medium), or, in Great Britain, a blend of coffee and roast fig. "New Orleans Coffee" is usually a dark-roasted coffee mixed with chicory root, occasionally a dark-roasted Brazilian blend *without* the chicory.

Decaffeinated, or caffeine-free coffees, have had the caffeine soaked out of them; they are sold to the roaster green like any other coffee. Roasters in most metropolitan centers will offer both a medium or American roast and a dark-roast decaffeinated bean. The provenance of the bean should still be designated: "Decaffeinated French-roast Colombian," for instance. Some roasters may carry as many as five or six decaffeinated straight coffees. The epithet "water-only" applied to decaffeinated coffee means the caffeine has been removed from the bean without the use of a solvent.

an insidious fad

In about 1978, an insidious fad crept off the instant-food shelves and slunk over into the specialty coffee section: This aberration is the "flavored" whole-bean coffee. Typically, either an inexpensive blend of beans or one of the less pricey Colombian coffees is sprayed with essential oils or smeared with other natural flavorings immediately after roasting, while the bean is cooling. The flavorings are absorbed into the bean. This gourmet parody appears to have crested in popularity, but consumers are still trailing into stores requesting "chocolate-rum coffee," "chocolate-mint coffee," or a dozen other flavors, presumably to serve with their wine coolers or canned cocktails. I wish I could say that this mutant came crawling out of Lake

Mead into Las Vegas, but apparently it surfaced in New York, where at least some people should know better.

But to cut the snobbish jokes and try to be helpful: If you buy any of these idiocies, try the chocolate. Avoid rum and brandy in particular; they taste decent when they're very fresh but develop the most rancid flavor imaginable when they're held on the shelf. And have these flavored coffees ground at the shop, or use your blade-style mill; they will gum up your burr grinder hopelessly.

Given a good quality bean, roasting is probably the single most important factor influencing the taste of coffee. The significant variable is the length of time the coffee is roasted. The longer the roasting, the darker the bean. The darker the bean, the more tangy and bittersweet the flavor. When this flavor settles onto the average coffee drinker's palate, he calls it "strong."

Now for our first plunge into the taste jungle, unarmed except for a dictionary. "Strength" in coffee properly refers to the proportion of coffee to water, not the flavor of the bean. The *more* coffee and the *less* water the *stronger* the brew. So you could make a light-roasted, mild-flavored coffee very *strong,* and brew a dark-roasted, sharp-flavored coffee very *weak.*

I would rather call this dark-roasted flavor "dark," "bittersweet," "tangy," "sharp," or maybe "European." Anything but "strong," since we need that word for later. This flavor comes in degrees, depending on how dark the bean is roasted, and eventually becomes virtually a new flavor when the bean is roasted entirely black. To understand the chemistry behind the change, one needs to know what happens when a coffee bean is roasted.

The green coffee bean, like all the other nuts, kernels, and beans we consume, is a combination of fats, proteins, fiber and miscellaneous chemicals. The aroma and flavor that make coffee so distinctive is present only potentially until the heat of roasting simultaneously forces much of the moisture out of the bean, and draws out of the base matter of the bean fragrant little beads of a volatile, oily substance variously called coffee

CHOOSING ROASTS

the dark-roasted flavor

fragrant beads

29

essence, coffee oil, and coffeol. This stuff is not properly an oil, since it (fortunately) dissolves in water. Beside dissolving in water, it evaporates easily, absorbs other less desirable flavors readily, and generally proves to be as fragile a substance as it is tasty. Without it there's no coffee, only sour brown water and caffeine, yet it constitutes only one two-hundredth of the weight of the bean.

The roasted bean is in a sense simply a dry package for this oil. In light or American-roasted coffee, the oil gathers in little pockets throughout the heart of the bean. As the bean is held in the roaster for longer periods and more moisture is lost, the oil is further developed, and begins to rise to the surface of the bean, giving the characteristic oily appearance of darker roasts.

Beneath the oil the hard matter of the bean develops a burned flavor, which adds the bittersweet undertone so attractive to dark-roast aficionados. Eventually, the bean virtually turns to charcoal and tastes literally burned; this ultimately roasted coffee is variously called dark French, Italian, or heavy roast, and has an unmistakable charcoal tang.

less acid   Darker roasts also contain considerably less acid and somewhat less caffeine than lighter roasts; these too go up the chimney with the roasting smoke. Consequently, dark roasts lack that slightly sour snap or bite coffee people call "acidy." Some dark-roast coffees taste bitter or sour, but this is owing to the cheaper coffees used in the blend rather than the roast, and such sourness should not be confused with either the dry snappy bite of a good acidy coffee, or the bittersweetness of a good dark roast.

Back to terminology for a moment. Coffee drinkers are so habitual that whole nations march from coffee initiation to grave knowing only one roast. This peculiar uniformity accounts for the popular terminology for describing *peculiar*   roasts: French roast and Italian roast, which vie for the darkest; Viennese or *uniformity*   light French, a slightly darker roast than American; and so on down to what we might call "American roast," which is by country lightest of all.

This assigning of national names to coffee roasts is a bit arbitrary, but based on sound fact that southern Europeans roast their coffee darker than

1	Light brown; dry surface.	Cinnamon New England Light	Tastes more like toasted grain than coffee, with distinct sour or acidic tones.
2	Medium brown; dry surface.	Regular American Medium high Medium Brown	For an American the characteristic coffee flavor; the grain flavor is gone; a definite acidy snap, but richer toned and sweeter than 1.
3	Slightly darker brown; patches of oil on the surface.	Light French High Viennese* City Full city	A slight, dark-roasted, bittersweet tang, almost indistinguishable. Less acidy snap than 2.
4	Dark brown; oily surface.	Italian Espresso European** French After-dinner Continental Dark	A definite bittersweet tang; all acidy tones gone.
5	Very dark brown, almost black; very shiny, oily surface.	Dark French French Italian Heavy	Burned or charcoal tones plus the bittersweet tang; all acidy tones gone.

*Viennese also sometimes refers to a blend of about one-third dark-roasted beans (4 or 5), and about two-thirds medium-roasted beans (2).

**European sometimes refers to a blend of about two-thirds dark-roasted beans (4 or 5), and one-third medium-roasted beans (2).

BUYING IT

northern Europeans or Americans. Whether the darkness of roast has some correlation to the relative intensity of nocturnal habits among the various nations of coffee drinkers, I'll leave to those who may want to consider this question over their second cup of dark-roast coffee.

names for roasts

The common terms for roasts among most coffee sellers are the standard, unnamed American roast (medium brown), Viennese or light French (slightly darker than American with the merest undertone of dark tang), Italian, espresso, or continental (dark brown, definitely dark flavored and bittersweet), and Italian or dark French (nearly black).

Your best bet is to learn to associate flavor with the color and appearance of the bean rather than with the name alone, but for reference I've condensed everything you'll need to know about the names of roasts in a table on the preceding page.

blending roasts

You can either buy a coffee roast as dark as you care to drink it, or make a blend of roasts. If you wish to blend roasts, buy a good, straightforward, acidy coffee like a Colombian, medium-roasted. Then begin adding French- or Italian-roasted beans, a few at a time, every time you grind yourself some coffee. Eventually, adding and subtracting, you'll arrive at proportions that please you and you can mix up your own blend, a half-pound at a time. Of course you may be the mercurial type who likes a different blend every time, in which case, carry on.

the next step

If you don't have a grinder, have the coffee-store clerk make a blend for you before grinding. I'd suggest you start with half dark-roast (the darkest) and half American-roast Colombian, and work the proportions up or down from there. The next step in determining your personal blend is to experiment with the light-roasted coffee; substitute some winey Kenya or heavy-bodied Sumatran for the Colombian, for instance. But for that, read on.

At this point a reader with a logical turn of mind might ask: Why don't specialty stores offer a whole line of dark-roasted straight coffees? Dark-roasted Colombian, for instance, dark-roasted Sumatran, and so on. A few coffees cannot be successfully dark-roasted; the bean is too soft and will become brittle and break apart if carried to too high a roast. Most coffees *can* be dark-roasted, and some roasters do offer a variety of dark roasts. Most do not, however. They argue that since dark roasting burns out many acids and other chemicals, with them go the subtle differences in flavor which distinguish one straight coffee from another. Thus it wouldn't be worth a specialty coffee roaster's effort to dark roast a variety of beans.

It is true that virtually all distinctions in flavor are burned out with a very dark, black-roasted preparation. But with the medium-dark roasts from categories 3 and 4 (see page 31), certain distinctions remain. Dark-roasted Kenya may not taste like Kenya anymore, but it will taste different from dark-roasted Colombian. Heavy-bodied coffees make heavy-bodied dark roasts, for instance. Some coffees dark-roast sweeter than others. Mexican, for example, makes a particularly sweet dark roast.

Also, roasters have different tastes in assembling their dark-roasted blends. Latin Americans, for instance, like a hint of sourness in their blends; it reminds them of the coffee their mamas made. So most dark-roasted coffees blended "for the Latin American taste" have a touch of the medicinal flavor called "Rioy." The same holds true for "authentic" New Orleans coffee, and some traditional, dark-roasted Italian espresso blends.

Once you learn to distinguish between roasts, you may want to pick out a dark-roasted *blend* which suits you best. Ask the clerk whether the dark-roast coffee he has for sale is a straight coffee or a blend. If it's a blend it may range from bitter to almost sweet, depending on the tastes of the *bitter to almost sweet* blender. The bitterness I'm describing here, of course, is a different matter entirely from the distinctive tang that comes from roasting coffee darkly in the first place. It is a quality of the coffee itself, rather than a flavor acquired through roasting.

And if you love dark-roasted coffee, in fact, if you love any kind of coffee, you may want to learn to roast your own. You can buy the best beans, roast them precisely to your taste, drink exquisitely fresh coffee always, and save considerable money.

3 TASTING IT
What to taste for; choosing coffee by country and market name

LEARNING TO DISTINGUISH roast is the first, relatively simple step in learning to taste and buy coffee intelligently. Once we move from roast to distinguishing coffees by country of origin, we enter a more ambiguous realm. Signs and brochures bombard us with light and full bodies, mellow, acidy, bright, and distinctive flavors, rich and pungent aromas, and on into the mellow, full-bodied tropical sunset. The bright-eyed assurance with which these terms are delivered shuts up everyone but people from Brooklyn and small children.

Most stores carry 15 to 30 varieties of straight coffee, all of which have to be described somehow or other on a sign or brochure. By the middle of the list you sense a certain strain; by the end the writer sounds desperate: "stimulating and vibrant," writes one; "an exotic coffee with a lingering aftertaste, full-bodied and provocative," writes another; "stands apart in its own special way," adds still another. Perhaps. Is the emperor wearing his new clothes? Do these coffees really taste different?

coffee brochurisms

They do. Differences stand out on a coffee-educated palate as clearly as sugar and salt. Experienced coffee tasters can distinguish the origin of most coffees in a blend simply by smelling and tasting. The problem is two-fold,

TASTING IT

and has to do with communication. First, the public doesn't understand coffee language, in other words, doesn't associate terms in the brochures with sensations in the mouth. Second, in their effort to make every coffee sound absolutely different from every other coffee, brochure writers often *mealy mouthed* resort to mealy mouthed romanticisms and gourmet-magazine clichés in *romanticisms* place of genuine description.

The comedian George Carlin once pointed out there is no name for the two little ridges under the nose. The world is full of unnamed phenomena, and the closer we get to the heart of what it means to be alive, the more unnameable things get. The subtle differences in flavor and aroma among coffees are as palpable as breathing, but if anything, seem too real to be easily named. One slings a word at a flavor and feels like a painter trying to copy a sunset with a tar brush. So we're back to the same old refrain: The only thing to do is taste.

TASTING IT   Coffee tasting is in many ways more crucial to buying quality coffee than wine tasting is to buying quality wine. The reason: Wine is labeled fairly specifically, whereas coffee is labeled outright vaguely. For instance, we can learn from its label that a given wine is from France, a country; from Beaujolais, a region; and from Moulin-à-Vent, a village in Beaujolais whose vineyards produce a particularly sturdy and rich red wine. Finally, the bottle tells us what year the grapes were grown and the wine bottled. Suppose, however, that one buys a coffee from Ethiopia. More than likely it will simply be labeled "Ethiopian." This tells us absolutely nothing, and would be analogous to simply labeling all wines from France, from the cheapest *vin ordinaire* to an aged Lafite-Rothschild, as "French."

limits of labels   Some specialty roasters might go further and label a coffee "Ethiopian Harrar." Harrar, like Beaujolais, is a region, so we're getting closer, and "Harrar" further indicates it is a plantation-grown coffee. But even the fanciest specialty roaster will not tell us more. We are seldom told what plantation or estate or cooperative or village a coffee comes from, even though this last may be the most important piece of information of all. Nor are we told how long the coffee has been held in warehouses before roasting.

So a wine book can be much more specific in its recommendations than can a coffee book: first, because wine labels are themselves more specific; and second, because coffee demands a closer collaboration from retailer and consumer, all the way from delivery in this country to the point of actually being drunk. A bottle of wine certainly can be affected by how it is stored, transported, and handled, but the fact remains it is packaged and ready to be enjoyed (at however remote a date) when it leaves the winery. But coffee is subject to three crucial operations—roasting, grinding, and brewing—by parties who are thousands of miles away from the tree where the bean originated. Thus, coffee even from the same crop and plantation may taste differently after having been subject to the tastes of different roasters, and a variety of grinding and brewing methods.

wine vs. coffee labels

And then, with coffee, there is always the question of whether it even *is* a Mexican Oaxaca Pluma, or a Yemen Mocha, or a Jamaican Blue Mountain. Particularly with the higher-priced coffees, a temptation extends all the way from the exporter through the importer to the roaster to substitute lower-priced or more readily available coffees for those represented in signs and brochures. Thus coffee thrusts the consumer into a more active, and possibly more satisfying, role than does wine, but frustrates those who might prefer memorizing to tasting.

more active role

Consequently, we must learn to taste. And when you move your trade to a new store, you should start tasting all over again, since your favorites may no longer be your favorites. Naturally, this only applies to stores who roast their own or obtain their coffee from different roasters. If you just move across town you may find you're buying from the same roaster, but under a different label. Perhaps I should say, ask questions first, and then start tasting.

There is no coffee-tasting ritual for the lay coffee drinker as there is for the wine drinker. Professional coffee tasters slurp it off a spoon, roll it

TASTING IT

around in their mouth, and spit it into a bucket, which isn't common after dinner behavior. I suggest when you're tasting you make coffee in your ordinary way, sample the aroma, taste a little black, and then, *drink* it. The professional taster is checking for defects as well as strengths of many coffees each day, whereas you simply want something that tastes good to you the way you drink it.

at the same sitting

You may well want to compare, however, some samples of various coffees at the same sitting so you have some idea of what coffee terminology actually describes. Remember that dark-roasting mutes or eliminates distinctions in flavor, so make certain you sample coffees that have been roasted to standard North American taste: light- to medium-brown. You'll either have to make some individual samples with a small pot or a one-cup filter cone, or else brew it the way professional tasters do. In either case, you want to use the same amount of each coffee, ground the same, and brewed identically. If you want to go professional, assemble a clean cup or shallow glass for each coffee to be sampled, a soup spoon, preferably silver plate, a glass of water in which to rinse your spoon between samplings, and something to spit into. Put one standard measure (two level tablespoons) of each coffee to be sampled, freshly and finely ground, in each cup; pour five ounces of near-boiling water over each sample. Part of the grounds will sink to the bottom of the cup, and part will form a crust on the surface of the coffee. At this point you will test each sample for aroma. Take the soup spoon, and leaning over the cup, break the crust. Virtually

forget your manners

stick your nose in the coffee, forget your manners, and *sniff*. The aroma will never be more distinct than at this moment. If you want to sample it a second time, lift some of the grounds from the bottom of the cup to the surface, and sniff again.

After you've broken the crust most of the grounds should settle to the bottom of the cup. Use your spoon to scoop up whatever remains floating on the surface and dump it into your ad hoc spittoon. Now take a spoonful of each coffee, lift it to a point just below your lips, and suck it violently into your mouth. Your purpose is to spray coffee all over your tongue in order to experience a single, comprehensive jolt of flavor. If you do it right you'll produce a loud, hissing jet-stream sort of noise, which will probably startle your cat but make your dog look friendly.

This spraying activity should give you a notion of flavor. Now roll the mouthful of coffee around your tongue, bounce it, chew it even. This *even chew it* exercise should give you a notion of both the body and acidity of your sample, concepts which I will attempt to define in a page or two. After all this—spit the coffee out. Continue this procedure until you can distinguish the qualities I discuss in the pages following. If your palate becomes jaded or confused, sip some cold water or eat a bit of bread.

In the next column you will find listed most of the straight coffees you will encounter in American specialty coffee stores. There are five lists. Each of the first three represents a family of coffees, the fourth combines a couple of loners, and the fifth gives some special categories under which straight specialty coffees are often sold. First are the Latin American coffees, characterized by a bright, brisk acidity and clean, straightforward flavor. The second list is the Arabian and African family of coffees, characterized by a distinctive winey acidity. Third are the coffees of the Malay Archipelago, which have both heavy body and a lower-toned, richer acidity. In each list I've put the most distinctive and famous coffees first. The fourth list puts a pair of coffees together which have nothing in common except their difference from all the other coffees of the world, and the fifth gives some categories of coffees distinguished by factors other than geography.

When you begin tasting I suggest you choose one coffee from each of the first three lists, if possible Mexican Coatepec or Oaxaca Pluma, Ethiopian

TASTING IT

Harrar, and Sumatran Mandheling. After you've made up three cups, begin smelling and tasting. You should eventually attempt to distinguish the following qualities:

acidity

Acidity: Taste those high, thin notes, the dryness the coffee leaves at the back of your palate and under the edges of your tongue? This pleasant tartness, snap, or twist is what coffee people call "acidy." It should be distinguished from "sour," which in coffee terminology means an unpleasant sharpness. The acidy notes should be very clear and bright in the Mexican, a little softer and richer in the Sumatran, and overwhelming in the Ethiopian Harrar. Aged coffees, and some coffees from Venezuela, Tanzania, and India, have little acidity and taste almost sweet.

An acidy coffee is somewhat analogous to a dry wine. In some coffees that "acidy" taste actually does become distinctively "winey"; the winey aftertaste should be very clear in the Ethiopian Harrar.

body

Body is the sense of heaviness, richness, thickness at the back of the tongue when one swishes the coffee around one's mouth. The coffee is not *actually* heavier, it just tastes that way. To introduce a wine analogy again: Burgundies and certain other red wines are heavier in *body* than clarets and white wines. In this case wine and coffee tasters use the same term for about the same phenomenon. The Ethiopian Harrar should definitely have the lightest body, and the Sumatran the heaviest, with the Mexican in the middle. If you can't distinguish body, try pouring milk into each. Note how the flavor of the heavy-bodied Sumatran carries through the milk, while the flavor of the Ethiopian dies away. If you do drink your coffee with milk, you should definitely buy a heavy-bodied coffee. If you're a black-coffee drinker you *may* (not always) prefer a lighter-bodied variety.

aroma

Aroma can't, strictly speaking, be separated from acidity and flavor. Acidy coffees smell acidy, and richly flavored coffees smell richly flavored. It is true, however, that some coffees, Colombian and Kona for instance, are more fragrant than others.

Flavor is the most ambiguous term of all. Acidity has something to do with flavor, and so do body and aroma. Some coffees simply have a fuller, richer flavor than others, whereas in others the acidy tang, for instance, tends to dominate everything else. One can also speak of a "distinctively" flavored coffee, a coffee whose flavor characteristics stand out in a crowd. Of the three coffees I suggested you sample, the Ethiopian is probably the most distinctive, the Mexican least distinctive, and the Sumatran the richest.

flavor

You will find many other epithets applied to flavor. "Mild" or "mellow" for instance. Mild-flavored coffees are usually low on acidity, but full-bodied and flavorful enough to be pleasant rather than bland. "Mild" is also used as an antonym to "harsh." Harshly flavored coffees are unpleasantly bitter, sharp, or irritating. There are also specialized coffee tasting terms to describe undesirable flavor characteristics: grassy, earthy, hidy, barnyard fermented, and so on. Presumably all the coffees you will be tasting will be superior, hence free from such defects.

COFFEE BY COUNTRY

The finest Mexican coffees come from the south of Mexico, where the continent narrows and takes a turn to the east. The state of Oaxaca occupies the western slopes of the central mountain range, and Veracruz the eastern. Fine coffees are produced in both states. The fine estate-grown coffees of Veracruz, particularly the best of those known as Altura ("High") Coatepec, are considered the best coffees produced in Mexico. The best washed coffees of Oaxaca State, Oaxaca and Oaxaca Pluma, run a close second. Other Veracruz coffees of note are Altura Orizaba and Altura Huatusco.

MEXICAN
Oaxaca Pluma, Coatepec

Don't expect any of these coffees to taste like the Mexican coffee you may have tasted while visiting rural Mexico, however. The brew most Mexicans drink is made from the natural or dry-processed coffees which have been passed over by the exporters; these cheaper beans are usually dark roasted and glazed with sugar. They make a sweet, heavy brew with a peculiar sour twist, which some visitors love and which turns others into temporary tea drinkers. If you have acquired a taste for such coffees, you must pursue it outside the confines of the specialty coffee store. Look for

TASTING IT

canned coffees from the southern United States, or coffees with Latino names sold in Puerto Rican, Mexican, or Cuban markets.

But the fine coffees of Mexico are a different matter. They are not among the world's greatest coffees, because they often lack richness and body, but at their best they are analogous to a good light white wine—delicate in body, with a pleasantly dry, acidy snap. If you drink your coffee black, and like a light, acidy cup, you will like the best Mexican coffees.

GUATEMALAN
Antigua, Coban

Guatemala's central highlands produce some of the world's best and most distinctively flavored coffees. The names to look for are "Antigua," from the countryside west of the old capital of Guatemala Antigua, and "Coban," from Alta Vera Paz, a district a hundred or so miles northeast of Antigua. Some shops may advertise their Guatemalan coffees by grade; the highest grades are "strictly hard bean," indicating coffees grown at altitudes of 4,500 feet or higher, and "hard bean," indicating those grown between 4,000 and 4,500 feet.

Both Antigua and Coban have a very distinct spicy, or better yet, smoky flavor which sets them apart from all other coffees. They are very acidy, and the spiciness or smokiness comes across as a twist to the acidy tones. In body, the finest Guatemalan coffees are medium to full, and rich in flavor. You will like Guatemalan coffees, especially Antigua, if you like their smoky, distinctive flavor, and a fairly rich cup.

EL SALVADOR

Although its recent misfortunes have presented plentiful opportunities for stirring journalism, coffee from El Salvador poses a contrasting problem for romantic writers of coffee brochures: One doesn't know what to say about it. The general consensus is that El Salvador coffee has a flavor somewhere between neutral and mild. One brochure calls it slightly sweet, which is about the most positive thing I've heard about it. I'd say El Salvador coffee has decent body but lackluster flavor. The best grade is labeled "strictly high grown."

Central America

MEXICO

MEXICO CITY   **JALAPA**
COATEPEC   VERA CRUZ
HUATUSCO
ORIZABA

OAXACA PLUMA
OAXACA
OAXACA PLUMA

COBAN

HONDURAS

GUATEMALA
GUATEMALA CITY   EL SALVADOR
ANTIGUA

EL SALVADOR

JINOTEGA
MATAGALPA
NICARAGUA
MANAGUA

TRES RIOS
TARRAZU
SAN JOSÉ
COSTA RICA

PANAMA

TASTING IT

NICARAGUAN
Jinotega, Matagalpa

At this writing, Nicaraguan coffee is not being imported into the United States because of differences between the American and Nicaraguan governments, although some old crop may still remain in coffee importers' inventories. Nicaraguan coffee may have become politically correct for the left, but in flavor it is still definitely a coffee for the silent majority, and presents still another challenge for the coffee describers. One brochure tells us it's like Mexican coffee, but different. In general, I find it as middle of the road as Salvador: decent, straightforward flavor, fairly acidy, with medium to light body. The districts of Jinotega and Matagalpa produce the best-known Nicaraguan coffees.

COSTA RICAN
Tres Rios, Tarrazu, Heredia, Alajuela

Costa Rican is a classically complete coffee; it has everything and lacks nothing. The best displays an exceptionally full body and robust richness. Good Mexican coffees are brisk; good Costa Rican coffees hearty.

Costa Rican coffee is grown primarily in the countryside surrounding the capital, San José. Four of the most famous coffees by district are Tres Rios, Tarrazu, Heredia, and Alajuela. Altitude may be a more important factor in determining flavor than district; "strictly hard bean" indicates a Costa Rican coffee grown above 3,900 feet; "good hard bean" 3,300 to 3,900. But again, don't become absorbed in names and grades. If the coffee you taste is rich and hearty, analogous to a good Burgundy, and you like it, it is a good Costa Rican coffee.

JAMAICAN
Blue Mountain, High Mountain

Jamaican coffee is a story of extremes: The lowland coffees of Jamaica are so ordinary they are seldom sold in the United States except as fillers for cheap blends. On the other hand, Jamaica's highland coffees rank among the world's best, and Jamaican Blue Mountain, however one defines that name, is the world's most celebrated, most expensive, and most controversial coffee.

Some years ago it was not entirely clear whether any high-quality coffee from the Blue Mountain district of Jamaica was entitled to be marketed as "Jamaican Blue Mountain," or whether the name properly applies only to coffees grown on a single plantation, the Wallensford Estate. Today, responsible roasters designate estate-produced coffees grown at over 3,000 feet in the Blue Mountain district of Jamaica as authentic Blue Mountain. Most will be either Wallensford (best) or Silver Hill Estate Blue Mountain. If you want to know where a store's "Blue Mountain" comes from, you can always ask. Jamaica High Mountain properly describes a somewhat lesser coffee than Blue Mountain, grown at lower altitudes in other parts of the island.

Wallensford Estate

The Jamaican government complicated matters in recent years by insisting that the premium Jamaican coffees leave Jamaica in *roasted* form only, in order to maximize foreign exchange and create jobs for Jamaicans. Anyone who has read this far knows that roasting and canning coffee, however carefully, is hardly the way to maintain quality. The Jamaican government is again allowing green coffee to leave the country, however, so it is currently possible to taste the Blue Mountain coffees as they should be tasted, freshly roasted.

The Jamaican situation also has been complicated by the many people who, in one way or another, are attempting to profit from the extraordinary prices demanded for Blue Mountain. In particular, other plantation owners in the high mountains of Jamaica are attempting to produce a coffee that will ride on the coattails of the original onto the palates and into the pocketbooks of the Americans and Japanese. These entrepreneurs appear honest and well meaning; less admirable, however, are the American roasters who market a "Blue Mountain Style" coffee that has the taste characteristics of Blue Mountain, but that may contain no actual Blue Mountain in it whatsoever.

on the coattails

TASTING IT

Only the palate knows. The original Wallensford Blue Mountain was a fine coffee, and remains so. Other high-grown coffees from Jamaica may be equally fine. If they're the real thing and haven't staled, they should be understated and balanced, a quintessential classic coffee with enough of everything: rich flavor and aroma, full body and moderate acidity in perfect, subtle balance. Most of the ordinary imitative coffees from Jamaica have the body and richness, but lack the acidity; they are smooth, well-bodied, moderately rich coffees deserving to be drunk, but not to be carried on about.

quintessential classic

Are even the best high-mountain Jamaicans worth the prices currently being asked? I would say probably not. Blue Mountain is a great coffee, but I prefer not to encourage still another minor, but embarrassing, chapter in the long history of vanity, snobbery, and the sacrifice of substance to pretense. Right now, I would advise you to buy Sumatran if you prefer a full-bodied mellow coffee; Kenyan if you like a full-bodied coffee with good, hair-raising acidity; and the best Costa Rican if you're looking for classic high-grown balance.

DOMINICAN REPUBLIC
Santo Domingo

Coffee from the Dominican Republic is often called Santo Domingo, after the country's former name, perhaps because "Santo Domingo" looks so romantic on a coffee bag, and "Dominican Republic" so pedestrian. Coffee is grown on both slopes of the mountain range which runs on an east-west axis down the center of the island. The best grade is simply "washed," and the coffees with the best reputation come from Bani, Ocoa, and Cibao.

Another middle-of-the-road coffee: fair to good body, pleasant but not overbearing acidity.

HAITIAN

Haiti, which shares the island of Hispaniola with the Dominican Republic, has a coffee industry built on paradox. On the one hand, most of its coffee is raised on tiny peasant plots and processed by the most primitive of methods. On the other, the Haitian government has promulgated an extra-ordinarily detailed set of laws and prohibitions apparently intended to upgrade coffee quality by sheer force of edict.

The best of the many grades is "strictly high grown washed"; second best is "high grown washed." The heavy rainfall and deep volcanic soil coupled with the low altitudes may account for the mellow sweetness which distinguishes the best Haitian coffee. It has fair body and acidity to go with the pleasantly soft, rich flavor.

A coffee for sentimental adventurers.

The Colombian coffee industry is the giant of the "mild," or fine, coffee-producing countries of the world. Although it ranks second to Brazil with 12 percent of the world's total coffee production to Brazil's 30 to 35 percent, most of Colombia's 12 percent is great coffee, grown at high altitudes on small peasant holdings, carefully picked, and wet-processed.

COLOMBIAN
Medellín,
Armenia, Manizales

Central Colombia is trisected from north to south by three *cordilleras,* or mountain ranges; the central and eastern *cordilleras* produce the best coffees. The principal coffees of the central *cordillera,* going from north to south, are Medellín, Armenia, and Manizales, all named for the towns or cities through which they are marketed. Medellín is the most famous coffee of the three, known for heavy body, rich flavor, and fine, balanced acidity; Manizales and Armenia are in general thinner in body and less acidy. For the purposes of large-scale marketing in the United States, these three coffees are often grouped together as MAMs, an acronym for Medellín-Armenia-Manizales. If your coffee seller is not clear about the precise provenance of his Colombian coffee, it was probably sold as a MAM, which means it could be any of the three.

The two most famous coffees of the eastern *cordillera* are Bogotá, from the region surrounding the capital city of Colombia, and Bucaramanga, marketed through the town of the same name. Bogotá is considered one of Colombia's finest coffees, less acidy than the Medellín, but equally rich and

Bogotá, Bucaramanga

47

TASTING IT

flavorful. The Bucaramanga is a soft-bean coffee, with some of the character of fine Sumatran coffees: heavy body, low acidity, and rich flavor tones.

The highest grade of Colombian is "supremo." But again, to simplify matters for the commercial coffee buyers, the Colombians throw together two grades of coffee, supremo, and the second best, "extra," plus caracol or peaberry of both grades, into one more comprehensive grade, "excelso."

In recent years, Colombia has been replacing the original Bourbon strain of arabica with a faster-growing and heavier-bearing strain. These new trees produce a smaller bean, which many roasters and importers feel is inferior to the classic Colombian coffees from the Bourbon strain. Although tasting against a memory is tricky, I would tend to agree.

Nevertheless, Colombian coffee at its best, like Costa Rican or the best Kona, is a classic. No quality is extreme: This coffee is generally full-bodied, but not so full-bodied as Sumatran; acidy but not nearly so acidy as Ethiopian or Kenyan; richly flavored but not quite so rich as Sumatran or the best high-mountain Jamaican. The best Colombians even have a slight winey tone reminiscent of African coffees, but these winey tones are elusive and never dominate.

VENEZUELAN
Maracaibo, Caracas,
Mérida, Cúcuta

At one time, Venezuela ranked close to Colombia in coffee production, but since the discovery and exploitation of petroleum Venezuela seems to have relegated coffee to the economic back burners. Today Venezuela produces less than one percent of the world's coffee, and most of it is drunk by the Venezuelans themselves.

The best Venezuelan coffee comes from the far western corner of the country, the part which nestles up to Colombia. Coffees from this area are called Maracaibos after the port through which they are shipped, and include one coffee, Cúcuta, which is actually grown in Colombia, but shipped through Maracaibo. Coffees from the coastal mountains farther east are generally marked Caracas, after the capital city, and shipped through Caracas' port, La Guaira.

CUBA

JAMAICA

HAITI

DOMINICAN REPUBLIC

PUERTO RICO

HAITIAN

BLUE MOUNTAIN

SANTO DOMINGO

Caribbean
&
Upper South America

PANAMA

MARACAIBO

CARACAS

CARACAS

TRUJILLO

MÉRIDA

CÚCUTA

TACHIRA

COLOMBIA

BUCARAMANGA

VENEZUELA

MEDELLÍN

ARMENIA

MANIZALES

BOGOTÁ

BOGOTÁ

ECUADOR
ECUADOR

South America

PERU
CHANCHAMAYO
LIMA

BRAZIL

SANTOS
RIO
SÃO PAULO
RIO DE
SANTOS JANEIRO

PARANA

The best-known Maracaibo coffees are Mérida, Trujillo, Tachira, and Cúcuta. Mérida is the most distinctive, and most likely to be found in North American specialty stores. Trujillo is rather lifeless, only a step above the cheap Brazilian coffees. Tachira and Cúcuta are a group in themselves, since their rich acidity makes them resemble Colombian coffees.

The most characteristic Venezuelan coffees, in surprising contrast to the neighbor coffees from Colombia, are strikingly low in acidity. At worst they are spiritless, at best sweet and delicate. The best, like the Méridas, have fair to good body, and an unemphatic but pleasant flavor with hints of richness.

A good coffee to balance sharply acid coffees in blends, and a comfortable coffee drunk straight.

Ecuador, next country south from Colombia along the Andes, produces substantial amounts of coffee, but little seems to appear in North American specialty stores. Another unremarkable coffee, thin to medium body, with occasional sharp acidity.

ECUADOR

Coffee from the Chanchamayo Valley, about 200 miles east of Lima in the high Andes, has the best reputation of the Peruvian coffees, and is more than likely the source for the "Peruvian" at your specialty store. Generally a mildly acid coffee, thin-bodied, but flavorful; resembles the lesser Vera Cruz coffees of Mexico.

PERUVIAN
Chanchamayo

When not suffering catastrophic frosts, Brazil produces something like 30 to 35 percent of the world's coffee. Vast plantations of millions of trees cover the hills of south-central Brazil. For the commercial coffee industry Brazil is of supreme importance, a giant in every respect; but for the specialty coffee trade it shrinks to something smaller than El Salvador. For of all the coffee produced in Brazil, none ranks close to the world's best. The Brazilian coffee industry has concentrated from the beginning on producing "price" coffees: cheap, fairly palatable, but hardly distinguished.

BRAZILIAN
Santos, Bourbon Santos

TASTING IT

There are four main coffee-growing regions in Brazil; only one, Santos, is of any importance for the specialty coffee trade; another, "Rio," is significant mainly because it gives its name to a peculiar medicinal flavor which coffee people call "Rioy."

Santos coffees are grown mainly in the state of São Paulo. In the 19th century, Rio coffee's harsh flavor competed in favor with the mild Santos. Much of the famous New Orleans coffee was Rio coffee, with chicory added, and some coffees dark roasted in the United States today for the "Latin taste" may still add Rio coffee to their blend. This is because Latins, who drank the cheap, Rioy-tasting natural coffees at home while the more expensive, washed milds were being sold to the United States, may still crave a bit of the old home-country harshness in their dark-roasted blends, even though they now live on the richer side of the Tropic of Cancer.

Santos coffee, named for one of the principal ports through which it is shipped, comes mainly from the original "Bourbon" strain of *Coffea arabica* brought to Brazil in the 18th century from the island of Bourbon, now Réunion. For the first three or four years these trees produce a small, curly bean which coffee people call "Bourbon Santos." This is the highest-grade coffee Brazil produces, and it will more than likely be the coffee your store sells as "Brazilian." After three or four years the beans begin to grow flat and larger; this coffee is called "flat bean Santos" and is cheaper and less desirable than the Bourbon Santos.

In flavor Bourbon Santos is smooth, in body medium, with moderate acidity; in short, another decent but hardly extraordinary coffee. Since it generally sells for about the same as more distinguished, unusual coffees, I see little reason to buy it except gourmet curiosity. Occasionally one sees the cheaper Brazilian coffees for sale in specialty stores, presumably to be used by the consumer to save money in his private blends.

MOCHA
Yemen, Arabian

"Mocha" is one of the more confusing terms in the coffee lexicon. The coffee we call Mocha today is grown as it has been for hundreds of years in

the mountains of Yemen, at the extreme southwestern tip of the Arabian peninsula. It was originally shipped through the ancient port of Mocha, which has since seen its harbor blocked by a sandbar. But the name Mocha has become so permanently a part of the world's coffee vocabulary that it stubbornly sticks to a coffee which would be more accurately described today as "Yemen" or even "Arabian."

The other ambiguity derives from Arabian Mocha's famed chocolaty aftertaste, which caused some enthusiast to name the traditional mixture of hot chocolate and coffee "mocha." So today "Mocha" is: an old-fashioned nickname for coffee, a common name for coffee from Yemen, Arabia, and the name of a drink made up of coffee and hot chocolate in equal parts.

Aside from the wild coffees of Ethiopia, Arabian Mocha is the most ancient and traditional of coffees, and still one of the best. It is the bean that literally sold the world on coffee. Yemen Mocha is still grown as it was in 600 A.D., on irrigated terraces clinging to the sides of semi-arid mountains; water is directed through little rock-lined channels to the roots of the plants, which are shaded from the desert sun by rows of poplars. The beans are also processed as they have been for centuries; even the best grades (Mocha extra) are "natural" coffees, dried with the fruit still attached to the beans. The dried husk is later removed by millstone or other primitive methods, which accounts for the rough, irregular look of the beans. The names in *Mattari, Sharki,* Yemen coffee are also irregular: No two authorities agree whether they *Sanani* properly indicate grade, district, or variety of bean. But all do agree that Mattari is the best Yemen Mocha, Sharki a close second, and Sanani third.

The plantation coffees of Arabia and Ethiopia, and some Kenya and Tanzania, are the most distinctively flavored coffees in the world. The acidity leaves an unmistakable dry, wine-like aftertaste on the palate. If Mexican coffees can be compared to dry white wines, Mochas and Ethiopians are the Bordeaux of the coffee world. In addition to its rich wininess, Mocha has its own particular flavor note, which some people, with more imagination than accuracy I think, associate with chocolate. Think of it as chocolate if you like, but don't be disappointed if it doesn't taste like Hershey's. It is a peculiar rich edge to the aftertaste that lurks very clearly but subtly behind the winey acidity. The stronger you make your coffee, the more clearly you will taste the "chocolate" flavor.

For the past several years Yemen Mocha, owing to the politics and quotas of the International Coffee Organization, has not been available regularly in the United States. We can reacquaint ourselves with this superb coffee, however, as it is becoming available again. If your store has been selling something called Mocha over the past few years, there is a good chance it was an Ethiopian Harrar rather than the true Yemen Mocha. The Ethiopian product is often an excellent coffee, but is not as rich or as balanced as the best Yemen.

politics and quotas

Since Mocha is such a distinctive coffee, everyone has something interesting to say about it: "unique," "sharp flavor," "mellow body," "creamy, rich," "distinctive winey flavor," etc. Despite its distinctiveness, I find it a very balanced coffee, with a medium to full body, good but not overwhelming acidity, and a rich flavor with those tantalizing "chocolate" undertones. Its aroma is overwhelming and delicious, heady with tantalizing winey and acidy notes.

A fine coffee. If you think they all taste the same, try this one.

Coffee was first cultivated across the Red Sea in Yemen, but the arabica tree originated on the mountain plateaus of Ethiopia, where tribesmen still harvest the wild berries. The coffee which is usually sold in the United States as "Ethiopian," however, is grown on plantations near the old capital of Harrar or Harari, at about 5,000 to 6,000 feet. You will see it called "Ethiopian Harrar," "longberry Harrar" (large bean), "shortberry Harrar" (smaller bean), or "Mocha Harrar" (peaberry); the "Harrar" may also become "Harari" or "Harar." In Great Britain Harrar is universally sold as "Mocha," adding to the confusion surrounding that abused term.

ETHIOPIAN
Harrar, Jimma, Abyssinian

TASTING IT

Ethiopian Harrar is the winiest coffee in the world; you may think someone's spiked your cup with Chianti. The winey quality that some Colombians hint at and that clearly comes through in Mochas, totally *strong and gamey* triumphs in Ethiopian Harrars. The wininess is strong, gamey, like a rough, dry, light, country red wine. Harrar has a light body, however, much lighter than Mocha, and more acidity, which means it lacks Mocha's mellow balance.

A coffee for people who like excitement at the cost of subtlety, those with dull palates, or a craving for the unusual.

Other coffees of Ethiopia, however, exhibit alternate extremes of flavor. Washed coffees from some Ethiopian estates often show little sign of the characteristic gamey wininess of their compatriot coffees. Instead these are gentle and rich, much like Indonesian coffees, and may exhibit floral or perfumey tones. These may be sold as Ethiopian Sanani, Ethiopian Estate Grown, or Ethiopian Fancies. And the wild coffees of southeastern Ethiopia, which are gathered rather than cultivated, are still another matter. They are carelessly picked, processed by the dry method, and at best are bland. You will probably not run across them in your specialty store. They are sold in the trade as Ethiopian or Abyssinian or by district as Jimma or Djimmah.

Although Kenya is only a few hundred miles south of Ethiopia and Yemen, coffee growing came late here. The native Kenyans have taken up what the Germans started and the British perfected, and made the East African coffee industry possibly even more modern and efficient than the Colombian. The coffee is raised both on small peasant plots and on larger plantations.

The main growing area stretches south from the slopes of 17,000-foot Mt. Kenya almost to the capital, Nairobi. There is a smaller coffee-growing region on the slopes of Mt. Elgon, on the border between Uganda and Kenya. Most Kenya coffee sold in specialty stores appears to come from the central region around Mt. Kenya, and is sometimes qualified with the name of the capital city, "Nairobi." Grade designates the size of the bean; "AA" is largest, followed, of course, by "A" and "B."

Kenya, like the Arabian Mocha and the Ethiopian Harrar to the north, has a distinctive dry, winey aftertaste. At its best, however, it has a full-bodied richness that Ethiopian and even Mocha lacks. Furthermore, it is getting better, as growers respond to government incentives encouraging quality. A fine coffee for those who like the striking and unusual. Not so winey as Ethiopian Harrar, fuller-bodied, but more intense all around than the Yemen Mocha.

KENYA
Nairobi

Tanzania's coffee industry was at first closely tied to the Kenyan, since early in their national histories they shared common exploiters: first the Germans, then the British. Most Tanzania arabicas are grown on the slopes of Mt. Kilimanjaro and Mt. Meru, near the Kenyan border. These coffees are called "Kilimanjaro," or sometimes "Moshi" or "Arusha" after the main towns and shipping points. Smaller amounts of arabica are grown much farther south, between Lake Tanganyika and Lake Malawi, and are usually called "Mbeya," after one of the principal towns. In all cases the highest grade is "AA," followed by "A" and "B."

Most Tanzania coffees have the characteristically sharp, winey acidity

TANZANIA
Kilimanjaro, Moshi

typical of African and Arabian coffees. They tend to be medium to full-bodied, and fairly rich in flavor. Other arabicas from Tanzania have a totally different character, more akin to the coffees of Sumatra and Celebes: rich, full-bodied, very mellow, and not at all acidy, with hardly a trace of the winey bite of Africa.

An excellent coffee in either case. Something for everyone: a rich, mellow coffee for those who like comfort, and another bright, winey coffee for those who crave the exotic.

UGANDA
Bugishu

The main part of Uganda's production is robusta, used in instant coffees and as cheap fillers in blends. Uganda does produce one excellent arabica, however: Bugishu, from the western slopes of Mt. Elgon, on the Kenyan border. It is another typically winey African coffee, close to the Kenyan coffees in flavor, but lighter in body.

ZIMBABWE

Zimbabwe, formerly Rhodesia, has been exporting an excellent coffee to the United States in recent years. It is a washed plantation coffee and still another variant on the acidy, winey-toned coffees of East Africa. Some importers rank Zimbabwe with the best Kenyan coffees. Samples I have tasted were not so full-bodied or rich, but it is a fine African-style coffee, nevertheless.

MYSORE
Indian

Mysore is a state in southern India which grows most of India's arabica coffees. Specialty coffee sellers usually call this coffee "Mysore" after the state, rather than "Indian." Legend attributes the first coffee trees in India to a Moslem pilgrim, Baba Budan, who is supposed to have smuggled seven coffee seeds out of Mecca and brought them back to Mysore strapped to his belly around 1600. His seed flourished, but more than likely the Mysore coffee you buy now is from seed introduced later by the British. The best grades are "arabica plantation A and B," and "arabica cherry AB"; the best-known regional names are Baba Budan, Niligris, and Sheverays.

Indonesia & New Guinea

ANKOLA/MANDHELING
PADANG
SUMATRA

BORNEO
(KALIMANTAN)

MANADO
KALOSSI
CELEBES
(SULAWESI)
RANTEPAO

MAKASSAR

JAVA
JAVA ARABICA

NEW GUINEA

NEW GUINEA

TASTING IT

In general, I have found Mysore to be a fairly full-bodied coffee with low acidity, and rather lifeless in flavor and aroma. It strikes me as a coffee which might well mellow out a very acid coffee in a blend, but I wouldn't recommend it on its own. Those who like a mellow, low-acid coffee with heavy body would be better buying a Sumatran.

SUMATRAN
Mandheling, Ankola

Some of the most famous coffees of the world are grown on the gigantic islands of the Malay Archipelago: Sumatra, Celebes, and Java in Indonesia, and Papua New Guinea. While Central American coffees are distinguished by their dry, winey aftertaste, the coffees of Indonesia and New Guinea are noted for their richness, full body, and an acidity which, though pronounced, is deep-toned and gentle. They are perfect for those who want a coffee heavy enough to carry its flavor through milk. Indonesian coffees are leisurely. There is something warm and reflective about them; they remind me of gigantic meals and wicker chairs.

Many consider the Mandheling and Ankola coffees of Sumatra the world's finest. They are often hard to find, but still moderate in price. Of the two, Mandheling is the more admired. They are both grown near the port of Padang in west central Sumatra, at altitudes of 2,500 to 5,000 feet. Mandheling is probably the most full-bodied coffee in the world; you can feel the richness settling in the corners behind your tongue. It has a relatively low acidity, but enough to keep the cup vibrant and interesting. The flavor, like the body, is rich, smooth, and full.

A coffee for fulfilled romantics.

CELEBES
Sulawesi, Kalossi,
Rantepao

The island of Sulawesi or Celebes spreads like a four-fingered hand in the middle of the Malay Archipelago. Celebes Kalossi, another of the world's most famous coffees, is grown near the port of Manado, on the southern-most finger. The samples I have tasted make it very similar to Sumatran Mandheling, but possibly a little less rich and full-bodied, and a bit more acidy and vibrant in the upper tones. Coffee from the south of the island, marketed as Rantepao, is excellent, but less admired.

Another gourmet coffee for those who prefer richness and full body to brightness and dry snap.

The Dutch planted the first arabica trees in Java early in coffee history, and before the rust disease virtually wiped out the industry, Java led the world in coffee production. Most of this early acreage has been replaced by disease-resistant robusta, but arabica has made a mild comeback.

JAVA
Java Arabica

Java at its best is another full-bodied, rich coffee. It is perhaps a little more acidy than Sumatran or Celebes, with a slight smoky or spicy twist to the acidity. It is this quality which leads people to call it "pungent," "strong-flavored," or "spicy," though I find these descriptions overstated.

"Old Government," "Old Brown," or simply, "Old" Java describe Java arabica that has been held in warehouses for two to three years. Such "matured" coffee turns from green to light brown, gains body and sweetness, and loses acidity. Old Java was one of the world's great gourmet coffees until it disappeared from the market after World War II. It has recently been revived, although it remains difficult to obtain in the United States. Similar coffees are readily available in Great Britain, however, and visitors there should take the opportunity to sample them. Old Java is a fine variation on the Indonesian theme: heavy-bodied, rich, and darkly sweet.

Old Java

Coffee labeled "New Guinea" comes from Papua New Guinea, which occupies the eastern half of the island of New Guinea. These coffees are grown in peasant patches and small plantations throughout the rugged mountain highlands. The best New Guinea coffee is estate, or plantation grown. In general, New Guinea is a low-key version of the great Indonesian coffees: not as full-bodied as the best Sumatran, less acidy and aromatic than the best Celebes, but a comfortably rich cup.

NEW GUINEA

TASTING IT

KONA
Hawaiian

Kona, on the southwest coast of the biggest island of the Hawaiian chain, is the only significant coffee-growing district in Hawaii, although coffee is grown in smaller quantities elsewhere on the islands. In the Kona district, the trees are shaded by a cloud cover that appears like clockwork around two o'clock in the afternoon (the famous "automatic shade"), just in time to protect them from the full devastation of the tropical sun.

In years past, Kona appeared to be on the way to becoming a luxurious memory. A tourist-inflated economy, low coffee prices, and an aging population of grower-landowners appeared to be conspiring to doom the Kona coffee industry—not to mention that local schools no longer timed their vacations to coincide with the coffee-picking season. But that was before the 1977 coffee price hikes, before tourists discovered the romance of Kona coffee, and before a new generation of small, quality-oriented coffee producers appeared on the scene. The revival of Kona coffee is now in full swing, and this coffee, always excellent, appears to be improving.

In the process Kona has become a bit pricey, perhaps too pricey when compared to some of the world's great and undervalued coffees, like the best Sumatran, Guatemalan, and Kenyan. Nevertheless, it's American, it's romantic, and it's an excellent coffee: medium-bodied, fairly acidy, with some subtle winey tones, very richly flavored, and when fresh, overwhelmingly aromatic. If you like to tantalize yourself with coffee fragrance before you drink, or find Indonesian coffees too rich, African coffees too winey, and those of Central and South America too sharp, Kona may be the coffee for you. Best grade is Extra Fancy, followed by Fancy and Number One grades.

Maragogipe is a variety of arabica that produces a very large, rather porous bean. It is a mutant spontaneously produced in Brazil, almost as though the one-time sleeping giant of the Americas thought regular beans were too puny and produced something in its own image. It was first discovered growing near the town of Maragogipe, in the southeastern state of Bahia. Subsequently it has been carried all over the world, and generally adopts the flavor characteristics of the soil to which it has been transplanted.

MARAGOGIPE

Opinions differ about the special qualities of the Maragogipe. William H. Ukers, one of the world's great authorities on coffee, found it tasted "woody and disagreeable" in 1928. Others have called it "the finest coffee known," and claim it will have a heavier body than a comparable arabica coffee from the same region. I've compared a Guatemalan Maragogipe with other Guatemalan arabicas and found it less acidy, lighter in body, and flatter in flavor. This last test is hardly conclusive, however, since the Maragogipe I tried may have come from lower altitudes than the arabicas. Like any other straight coffee, Maragogipes should be sold by country of origin.

Peaberry, or caracol, is a grade of coffee, rather than a botanical variety. All over the world the coffee fruit occasionally produces a single, rather than double, bean. This loner grows to be small and round, with a tiny crevice splitting it halfway down the middle.

PEABERRY

Coffee folklore has it that peaberry grades are superior to normal grades from the same crop, apparently on the basis that the good stuff that ordinarily goes into two beans goes into only one bean in the case of the peaberry. If anything, however, coffee from peaberries tends to be lighter in body and flavor than coffee from high-grade normal beans from the same trees.

Peaberry coffee should be sold by country and market name like any other coffee. If you see a sign that simply says "Peaberry," you should inquire as to the coffee's origin.

AGED COFFEES

As it ages green coffee loses acidity and, depending on how it is stored, gains body. Coffee delivered for roasting soon after harvest and processing is called "new crop." Coffee which has been held in warehouses for a period before delivery is called "old crop." "Mature" coffees are usually two to three years old. Aged or "vintage" coffees, which have been held in dry and well-ventilated warehouses for six to 10 years, constitute a fourth category. Under these conditions the acidity disappears entirely and is replaced by a peculiar syrupy richness. In general, coffees with full body and robust flavor age better than the more delicate growths.

At present few aged coffees are available; aging coffees represents a long-term capital investment most contemporary exporters are unwilling to take. One occasionally sees aged Venezuelan and Colombian coffees for sale in specialty stores, however, and aged Sumatran and Celebes are available, but seldom sold as straight coffees. You ought to try an aged coffee at least once; you will immediately note a rather dull, sweet heaviness, not at all like the more stimulating richness of a full-bodied new crop coffee or the still-lively sweetness of a "mature" coffee.

If you are anti-acidity to the point of fanaticism, you might like a straight aged coffee. They are most useful, however, in blends to give body and sweetness to "young," dry, sharply acid coffees.

BLENDING YOUR OWN

Since blending is the ultimate proof of coffee expertise, and since it gives the consumer a chance unusual in today's marketplace to participate in the creation of his own pleasure, specialty coffee customers often take to blending their own coffees. The only drawback to such a pleasant practice is impatience: The consumer may decide to begin blending before he knows enough to do it right, and the seller may get frustrated if he has to stop to make a blend of five coffees for a customer when there are 10 more customers waiting in line behind him. But let's let the seller take care of himself. Few storekeepers will object if they feel the customer is really blending, rather than just showing off or demanding attention, and it's your money anyhow.

One can blend different roasts, coffees with different caffeine contents, or straight coffees from different countries. One of the more common practices is to blend dark and light roasts, a procedure I discuss in detail in Chapter 2. Another reason to blend is to cut caffeine content. If you drink only decaffeinated coffee you may get bored, since specialty shops carry at most two caffeine-free coffees. If you drink only straight coffee you may get insomnia. An excellent compromise is to blend a caffeine-free coffee with your favorite straight coffees, thus cutting your caffeine intake while maintaining your spirit of adventure.

blending roasts

The art of blending straight coffees of the same roast is a subtler business, but hardly difficult once the basic principles are understood. Blenders who work for large commercial coffee companies need to be highly skilled because their job is more complex than ours. All we want to do is blend a coffee that suits us better than a single straight coffee would, taken alone. But the commercial blender also blends to cut costs while keeping quality up, and wants to assemble a blend that always tastes the same even though the straight coffees that make up the blend may differ. Certain coffees are not available at all times, some coffees may be cheaper than others at certain times of the year, and so on. But in an economy dominated by highly advertised brand names the blend has to taste more or less the same every time. So the blender may at times find himself tap dancing at the center of a shifting kaleidoscope of prices and availabilities, constantly juggling coffees in an attempt to keep the taste the same and the cost down.

blending straight coffees

A good commercial blend takes a fresh, sharp, acidy, aromatic coffee like Colombian, Costa Rican, or Mexican, and combines it with a decent grade of Brazilian coffee to cut costs. If it's a very high-priced blend, the blender might combine more than one quality coffee with the Brazilian: a rich, full-bodied coffee to balance a bright, acidy coffee for instance. Low-cost blends might decrease the proportion of mild coffee and Brazilian, and make up the difference with a very bland and inexpensive robusta. The very cheapest blends eliminate the high-priced mild coffee entirely, and simply combine a decent grade of Brazilian with the robustas.

Specialty coffee roasters usually have their own blends. A small roaster may have only one, his "house blend," or he may have as many as a half-dozen for all pocketbooks, tastes, and times of day.

less to consider

The consumer who makes his own blends has less to consider than the commercial blender. He shouldn't have to worry about consistency, and he can't use blending to bring the price down much, since most straight coffees sold through specialty stores are already premium coffees with premium prices. It would be like trying to save money by cutting caviar with truffles, or mixing 110 octane gas with 100 octane gas. Commercial coffee concerns can save money on their blends because they are able to buy large quantities of cheap coffee at bargain prices. As I indicated in Chapter 4, a more effective way to save money would be to buy green coffee in bulk and learn to roast it yourself.

principle of blending

So all you will be blending for is taste. The way to go about this is simple: You combine coffees which complement one another with qualities the others lack. The world's oldest and most famous blend, for instance, combines Arabian Mocha and Java. Part of the reason for its fame is of course tradition: It began when Mocha and Java were the only coffees available. Nevertheless, it embodies the sound principle of balancing extremes, or complements. Remember that Mocha is a mildly acidy, winey coffee with a fairly light body; Java is a heavier-bodied coffee, sweeter and deeper-toned. Put together they make a brew which is both less and more—less striking and distinctive, but more balanced and comprehensive.

Your first, and pleasurable, task in assembling a personal blend is to learn to distinguish acidity, body, and flavor in coffee, and possibly some of the more individual quirks: the dry aftertaste of African coffees, the smoky tones of Guatemalan Antigua. By then you should also know what qualities you prefer in a coffee, and what to blend for. You may simply want an all-around coffee, with the best of all worlds, or you may want a basically heavy, mellow coffee with only a little acidy brightness, or a brisk, light coffee with plenty of body, too.

But always proceed the same way. If you have a favorite coffee which seems to lack something, combine it with a coffee that has in extreme form *recommendations* what your favorite lacks:

- For brightness, snap, acidity, add Costa Rican, Colombian, Guatemalan, or any of the good Central American coffees.
- For body and richness, add Sumatran Mandheling, Celebes Kalossi, or Java.
- For sweetness, add Venezuelan Maracaibo or Haitian.
- For even more sweetness, or to dull a bright coffee, add an aged coffee or a Mysore.
- For flavor and aroma, add Kona, Jamaican Blue Mountain, Sumatran, Celebes, Guatemalan, or Colombian.
- To add a winey note, make the acidy coffee an Ethiopian; to add richness as well, make it a Kenya or Mocha.

The only real mistake one can make in blending is to combine two coffees which are distinctive or extreme in the same way. Two coffees with *blending friends* sharp, winey acidity like a Kenya and an Ethiopian, for example, would *and enemies* make a poor blend. Better combine an Ethiopian with a richer, low-key coffee like a Mysore. One has to be particularly beware of the distinctive, gamey coffees of Africa, which may make a dissonant blend with other acidy coffees. On the other hand, some coffees like Mysore or most Venezuelans, are so congenially understated that they get along with everybody. Others, like Mocha and the large Latin American family of coffees, are easy-going individualists who manage to get along with almost everybody, yet still maintain their distinction.

BLENDING
WITH CHICORY
AND FIG

Dark-roasted coffee is sometimes blended with chicory, particularly in northern France and the southern United States. Chicory is an easily grown, disease-resistant relative of the dandelion. The young leaves, when used for salad, are called endive. The root resembles the dandelion root, and when dried, roasted, and ground, produces a deeply brown, full-bodied, almost syrupy beverage which has a bitter peppery tang, and doesn't taste at all like coffee. In fact, it tastes like someone put some pepper in your herbal tea mixture. It is almost impossible to drink black; sweetened with milk it makes a fairly satisfying hot beverage, though it leaves a bitter, cloying aftertaste.

first use

According to Heinrick Jacob in *Coffee: The Epic of a Commodity*, some Germans first exploited the use of chicory as a coffee substitute around 1770. The Germans, who are probably more suspicious of the skeptical, sober, Apollonian effects of caffeine than any other nation, adopted chicory because it had no caffeine and (possibly most important) because it eluded the tariffs imposed on foreign luxuries like coffee. Jacob describes the trademark on 18th century packets of chicory: "A German farmer sowing chicory seed, and waving away ships freighted with coffee beans. Beneath was the legend: 'Without you, Healthy and rich.'"

But it was under Napoleon's "continental system," a sort of reverse blockade aimed at cutting England off from its European markets and making conquered Europe self-sufficient, that chicory came into its own. The French developed the sugar beet to replace sugarcane, but the chicory root was the best they could come up with for coffee. Not much of a substitute, since it has neither caffeine nor coffee's aromatic oils. After the collapse of the Napoleonic empire, the French went back to coffee, but never totally lost their taste for chicory.

The famous New Orleans-style coffee, which came to the southern United States with the French colonists, tastes the way it does for three reasons: it has chicory in it, the beans are dark roasted, and some cheap, naturally processed Brazilian beans are added to give the brew that old-time sour twist. If you like New Orleans-style coffee and want to carry your taste to more refined levels, you need to first determine which components account for what you like about the flavor: the chicory, the dark roast, or the sour beans.

New Orleans coffee

I assume by now you've tried dark-roast coffee. Next, buy ground French chicory, sold at most large specialty coffee stores. It costs a little less than coffee, and goes farther, which is another reason for developing a taste for New Orleans-style coffee. Now simply experiment by varying the proportions of chicory to ground dark-roast coffee. About 10 percent chicory will barely effect flavor, but will considerably increase the body and darkness of the brew. You get the peppery taste clearly at 20 percent, but it still doesn't overpower the coffee flavor, and you can drink such a blend black with pleasure. Most New Orleans blends are 30 to 40 percent chicory. At these proportions the bitter chicory flavor at least equals the coffee flavor, and I think most people would have trouble drinking such a blend black.

percentages

If you mix chicory and dark-roast coffee and it still doesn't taste as good to you as the canned commercial New Orleans blends, then it's the cheap natural beans you like, and you probably can't buy them unless you find a Latin American roaster who will let you have some green.

In Great Britain, a blend of coffee and roast ground fig is popular. Fig has a flavor very different from the heavy, peppery bite of chicory. Mixed in proportions of one part fig to seven parts ground coffee, fig adds considerable body and a delicate, fruity sweetness to the cup. I much prefer it to chicory, but since it's unavailable commercially in the United States and most readers will hardly bother to roast and grind it themselves, I won't carry on about it.

4 ROASTING IT
How coffee is roasted and how to roast your own

S INCE WE HAVE COME to associate the word coffee so absolutely with a hot, aromatic brown liquid, some may find it hard to believe that mankind had to fuss for several hundred years before concluding that the most interesting way to get what it wanted from the coffee tree was to roast the dried kernel of the fruit, grind it, and toss the resulting powder into hot water. The alternative solutions are many, and some still survive as part of the cuisine of Africa and Asia. The berries can be fermented to make a wine, for example, or the leaves and flowers cured and steeped in boiling water, to produce a coffee tea. In parts of Africa people soak the raw beans in water and spices, and chew them like candy. The raw berries are also combined with bananas, crushed, and beaten to make a sort of raw coffee and banana smoothie.

The key to the victory of the current mode of coffee making is the roasting process, to which we owe the delicately flavored oils that speak to the palate as eloquently as caffeine to the sleep-numbed nervous system. "The coffee berries are to be bought at any Druggist," says a 17th century English pamphlet on coffee drinking, "about three shillings a pound; take what quantity you please and over a charcoal fire, in an old pudding pan or

delicate oils

ROASTING IT

frying pan, keep them always stirring til they be quite black, and yet if you exceed, they do you waste the Oyl, which only makes the drink; and if less, they will it not deliver its Oyl, which must make the drink."

We may not agree with the Englishman's taste in roasting ("quite black" sounds more Neapolitan than English), but he knew what counted: The breaking down of fats and carbohydrates into an aromatic, volatile, oily substance which alone produces coffee flavor and aroma. Without roasting, the bean will give up its caffeine, acids, even its protein, but not its flavor.

chemistry The chemistry of coffee roasting is complex, and still not completely understood. This is owing to the variety of beans, as well as the complexity of the coffee essence, which is kinky enough to still defy chemists' best efforts to duplicate it in the laboratory.

Much of what happens to the bean in roasting is interesting, but irrelevant: The bean loses a lot of moisture, for instance, which means it weighs less after roasting than before (a fact much lamented among penny-conscious commerical roasters). It loses some protein, about 10 to 15 percent of its caffeine, and traces of other chemicals. Sugars are burned or caramelized, which contributes color and some body to the cup.

simple in theory Roasting is simple in theory: The beans must be heated, kept moving so they don't burn or roast unevenly, and cooled (or "quenched") when the right moment has come to stop the roasting. Coffee which is not roasted long enough or hot enough to bring out the oil will have a pasty, nutty, or bread-like flavor. Coffee which is roasted too long or at too high a temperature will be thin-bodied, burned, and industrial-flavored; very badly burned coffee will taste like old sneakers left on the radiator. Coffee roasted too long at too low a temperature will have a baked flavor.

Most roasting equipment uses a rotating drum with a heat source under it, usually a gas flame. The whole effect is a lot like a laundromat clothes drier. The rotating drum tumbles the beans, assuring an even roast. The air temperature inside the drum is usually controlled at about 500°F; for the first five minutes, the bean merely loses "free" moisture, moisture which is not bound up in the cellular structure of the bean. Eventually, however, the deep "bound" moisture begins to force its way out, expanding the bean and producing a snapping or crackling noise. So far, the color of the bean has not appreciably changed (it should be a light brown), and the oil has not been volatilized. Then, when the interior temperature of the bean reaches about 400°F, the oil quite suddenly begins developing; chemists call this process pyrolysis; it is marked visually by a darkening in the color of the bean.

pyrolysis

This is the moment of truth for the coffee roaster, machine or human, because the pyrolysis, or volatilization of the coffee essence, must be stopped at precisely the right instant to obtain the flavor and roast desired. The beans cannot be allowed to cool of their own accord, or they may over-roast. They are quickly dumped into a metal box, where pyrolysis continues until "quenched" with either cold air or a light spray of cold water. Most specialty roasters air-quench their coffee.

The exact nature of the roasting equipment depends on the ambitions of the roaster. Let's start with a big-time commercial roaster, work our way down through a small, store-front roaster, and from there to you and me in our kitchens. The coffee bean, when delivered to the roaster in big burlap sacks, ranges in color from light brown to whitish green. The beans are always stored green; roasted whole beans begin to deteriorate in flavor within a week after roasting, and ground coffee may taste stale within an hour after grinding, whereas green coffee may even improve with age.

equipment

The large commercial roaster resembles a big screw rotating inside a drum; the screw works the coffee down the drum. By the time the coffee reaches the end of the drum it is roasted, and ready to be cooled by air or water. The temperature is controlled automatically, and there may even be equipment that monitors the temperature inside the beans, to assure uniform roast. Such roasters are called "continuous" roasters for obvious reasons and are inappropriate for specialty roasters for several reasons: they cost too much, roast too much at a time, don't permit direct control of the roasting process, and don't work very well for dark roasts.

commercial roasters

ROASTING IT

the batch roaster The average specialty roaster uses a "batch" roaster, which is simply a rotating drum with heat under it; when the coffee is ready the roaster dumps the "batch" of coffee into a metal box where it is cooled. These batch roasters may be as large around as four or five feet, or as small as a small trash can set on its side.

On the facing page you'll find a picture of a typical small batch roaster. The drum (A) tumbles the roasting coffee over the gas flame (B). The fan (C) sucks the smoke and chaff out of the drum. When the beans are dumped into the cooling box (D) and ready to be quenched, the fan is reversed, and cool air is forced back through the hot beans at D.

Roasters, like cooks and artists, tend to fall into two schools: those who depend on an abstract system and those who follow their eyes, ears, nose and intuition. A systematic roaster might roast all his coffees for the same period of time, for instance, but roast each at a different temperature depending on the color of roast he wants plus the bean's hardness, or resistance to heat. These temperatures, based on tests, would all be a matter of written record. Thus the roasting process in theory could be duplicated by anyone who could read and set dials.

an intuitive roaster For an example of an intuitive roaster, let me introduce the memory of the Graffeo coffee shop in San Francisco, locally famous for its rich, sweet espresso coffee. At that time the roasting was done in a small, old-fashioned batch roaster by John Repetto, the father of the present proprietor, and an intuitive roaster if there ever was one.

Three open bags of green coffee stood next to the roasting machine. Two contained coffees from South and Central America, one with lighter and one with heavier body; in the third bag was a mix of four or five sharp, distinctively flavored coffees: Arabian Mocha, Kenya, or Ethiopian, for instance. With a fine nonchalance, Mr. Repetto would scoop about equal parts of each into the rotating drum of the roasting machine, close the door, and turn up the flame. Thereafter he wandered around the store, waiting on

ROASTER

ROASTING IT

customers and following this timetable, which anyone who roasts coffee at home would be wise to follow as well:

One: Coffee smells like the sack (do something else for a while).

Two: Coffee smells like bread (do it closer to the roaster).

Three: The beans begin to crackle (prepare for action).

When he heard them crackle, Mr. Repetto knew the oil was developing and began checking the color of the beans by collecting a few with a little spoon-like implement called a "trier," which is stuck through a hole in the front of the roasting cylinder.

When the color was about medium brown (the shop sells mainly dark-roast coffee), he opened a door in the cylinder, and the beans tumbled out into the box in front of the roaster. Here the roasting continued inside the steaming, crackling beans while he stirred them and studied them for color. When they were dark brown ("the color of a monk's tunic"), he tripped a lever on the side of the fan box, forcing cold air up through perforations at the bottom of the box to stop the roasting process at exactly the correct moment.

"the color of a monk's tunic"

Much specialty coffee is roasted in similar fashion in similar old machines, some large, some small, most with a loveable early industrial-revolution look. Other specialty roasting firms, as I indicated, work on a much larger scale with more up-to-date equipment. I recall my disappointment when I revisited the Graffeo shop and found the old roasting machine holding up plants in the store window and John's son, Luciano, wearing a white smock and watching some dials on the front of a chrome box. This box I recognized as a Sivitz roaster, the creation of Michael Sivitz, a well-known technical writer on coffee who some years before had gone into the business of producing his own coffee roasting equipment based on a new principle. Rather than rotating the beans inside a cylinder, the Sivitz machine suspends the beans in a floating mass atop a rapidly moving column of hot air. Mr. Sivitz claims that his system, which prevents the beans from touching hot metal for longer than a moment, produces a more uniform roast than the traditional drum roaster.

Perhaps. The coffee tastes good from the new machine, and it tasted good from the old. One thing is certain: Buying from the person who roasts the coffee is your best assurance of a fresh coffee, and a good coffee.

Those who want to be absolutely certain their coffee is fresh—in fact, anyone who wishes to drink the absolutely best cup of coffee possible—should experiment with roasting their own coffee at home. Home roasting is very simple, and very quick. It takes about as much time and skill as cooking spaghetti, and is considerably simpler than other more fashionable back-to-basics activities, like baking your own bread or making your own beer. And any small mistakes in the roasting process are far offset by the advantages of freshness.

ROASTING YOUR OWN

Roasted, ground coffee is in the larger perspective as much a convenience food as instant coffee or frozen foods. Americans roasted their own coffee until late into the nineteenth century, and many people all over the world still do. Jabez Burns, inventor of the continuous roaster, the first modern production roaster, insisted that some of the best roasted coffee he ever tasted was done in a corn popper.

The physical requirements for roasting coffee correctly are very simple: the coffee needs to be kept moving in air temperatures of at least 400°F, and to be cooled at the correct moment.

People who roast coffee at home, being the isolated individualists they are, unconfirmed in their activity by newspaper articles or TV commercials, are usually convinced that their way is the only way. There are in fact many ways, but they divide into four main approaches: 1) inside the oven, 2) on top of the stove, 3) in a hot-air popcorn popper, and 4) in a small, commercially produced electric home roaster.

isolated individualists

ROASTING IT

In the Oven Approach This is, in my opinion, the best because 1) you can control the roasting temperature; 2) the oily, persistent smoke produced by roasting is contained and directed through the oven vent; and 3) you don't have to turn a crank, or otherwise hover over your roasting coffee.

The best in-the-oven technique involves spreading a thin layer of green coffee beans over a perforated surface, which allows the convection currents of the oven to flow through the beans and maintain an even roast. Palani Plantation (430 Nevada Avenue, Palo Alto, California 94301) markets foil pans (2 for $5) that work very well; you can roast about four ounces in each pan; put two in the oven at a time and you've roasted a half-pound of coffee. However, an ordinary vegetable steamer, the kind that has petallike edges and expands to fit inside a pot, works just as well.

In either case preheat the oven to about 425°F, *no lower*. Place the green coffee beans in the vegetable steamer or Palani Plantation pan, and spread evenly, about two beans deep. Place the steamer or pan in the oven, and set your kitchen timer at 10 minutes. Place some sample beans that have been commercially roasted to the darkness you prefer on the counter near the oven, to use as a color comparison.

Soon you will hear the beans crackling, which indicates that pyrolysis has begun. A pungent odor may escape from around the oven door; this is the smell of the roasting smoke. The crackling will continue; in about 10 minutes, or about a minute or two after the crackling begins, check the color of the beans. Continue to check every one to two minutes until the beans in the oven have achieved a color *slightly lighter* than the color of your preferred sample.

Remove *immediately* and place in the coolest spot in your kitchen; the beans will continue roasting from their internal heat for a couple of minutes, which is why you should be careful to remove them *before* they achieve the full color you are aiming for. If your roast is slightly scorched or more darkly roasted in some places than others, don't be alarmed. It should still taste much better than partly staled store-bought coffee.

On Top of the Stove Approach Some lovely, romantic stove-top coffee roasters are available but in many cases they demand an intuitive approach to roasting, since there is no reliable way I can figure out to monitor properly the temperature inside the roasting device. I suggest a cheaper and, in some ways easier, alternative: the old-fashioned stove-top popcorn popper. A crank on top of the device rotates two vanes inside the pan which maintain an even roast by pushing the coffee around. These old-timey looking items retail for anywhere from $10 to $20. If you buy one, make sure the fit between the vanes and the bottom of the pan is snug. The beans may hang up between the vanes and the bottom, making the crank hard to turn.

top of the stove

Assemble the following: the stove-top popcorn popper, an oven thermometer (the kind with a little metal stand), and some sample beans commercially roasted to your preference. *Don't even try this approach if you don't have a strong kitchen exhaust fan over your stove.* The smell of coffee smoke may be romantic the first time around, but it eventually gets stale in more ways than one.

a kitchen fan

You first need to experiment by placing the oven thermometer inside the roaster or popper and closing the lid. Check the temperature at different burner settings until you find one that maintains the air temperature inside the popper at between 450° and 500°F. (You will need to maintain a higher temperature than with the oven approach, since you lose a great deal of heat every time you open the top of the popper.) Make a note of the burner setting so that you don't need to repeat the procedure every time you want to roast coffee. Then remove the thermometer, place about five ounces of green beans in the popper, and hang around the kitchen, because you will need to turn the crank on top of the popper regularly. Turn it occasionally until the crackling starts, then constantly until the beans inside the popper reach a color just lighter than your sample beans. (Start peeking inside a minute or two after the crackling begins.) Remove the popper from the heat immediately and dump the beans in a bowl. *Never* let your beans roast unattended; terminally roasted beans are flammable.

ROASTING IT

ball roaster

The most common stove-top roasters are a modified version of the popcorn popper I described earlier: a covered pan with a crank on top. These roasters range from rather flimsy versions at around $20 to a solid cast-iron model at $100. Even more impressive looking is the old-fashioned ball roaster, available from Thomas Cara in San Francisco (517 Pacific Avenue, San Francisco, California 94133), in all copper at $60. Many of these roasters have a relatively small opening, however, so one would need to cram an oven thermometer through the opening and examine it with a flashlight to figure out how high the flame needs to be kept to maintain a proper roasting temperature of 410° to 450°F. Instead, one simply wings it. Start with the heat on medium low, and if you don't get the smoke and hear the crackling in 10 minutes, turn up the heat until you do. Make a note of the burner setting and proceed as above.

Hot-Air Popcorn-Popper Approach The hot-air popcorn poppers now on the market ($12 to $20) will roast about three ounces of green beans nicely. They will also blow chaff around your kitchen and fill it with smoke, so the powerful kitchen fan continues to be a necessity. Simply put the green beans in the popper, and *stand by* (it would be very easy to ignite forgotten, unattended beans). When the beans are a little lighter than your sample, dump them in a bowl.

hot-air popcorn popper

Michael Sivitz, coffee expert and hot-air roasting pioneer, markets a modified popcorn popper ($55) with an optional chaff collector (an additional $20). The Sivitz device has a switch that enables you to cool your beans with nonheated air. I have not tried this latest version of the Sivitz home roaster, but I suspect it works rather well. Order from Sivitz Coffee Company, 349 S.W. Fourth Street, Corvallis, Oregon 97333.

Small, Commercially Produced Electric Home Roasters Until recently Melitta marketed a small, inexpensive (around $50) electric roaster, which roasted three ounces of green coffee per session. A much better (and much more expensive) product has come on the market, however: the Sirocco roaster, made in West Germany. The Sirocco roasts six ounces of coffee at a time in a glass roasting chamber (which enables you to accurately monitor roast color), has an automatic cooling cycle, and disposable smoke and chaff filters. The Sirocco retails at about $140; the disposable filters are five cents each. If your retailer doesn't carry this roaster, order from Sirocco Gourmet Coffee System, Box 79571, Houston, Texas 77279.

Sirocco roaster

GREEN COFFEE IN STORAGE

5 GRINDING IT
Choosing a grind and a grinder

EVERY STEP of the transformation of green coffee into hot brewed coffee makes the flavor essence of the bean more vulnerable to destruction. Green coffees keep for years, with only a slow, subtle change in flavor. But roasted coffees begin to lose their flavor after a week, ground coffee an hour after grinding, and brewed coffee in mere minutes.

Traditional Arab culture still has the best solution: Roast, grind, brew, and drink the coffee on the spot, all in the same sitting. The process takes *the best solution* about a half-hour, however, so I don't expect that it will catch on with the young urban professional. Roasting your own coffee every three or four days is an excellent compromise, but most of us are too distracted to take that step either, and prefer to let others do our roasting for us.

Roasted, whole coffee beans keep fairly well. The bean itself is a protective package, albeit a fragile one. Stored in a dry, airtight container to prevent contamination or contact with moisture, roasted whole-bean coffee will keep its flavor and aroma almost perfectly for about a week. After two, it will still taste reasonably fresh, but the aroma will begin slipping; after three the flavor begins to go, and whole-bean coffee kept past a month, while still drinkable, will strike the palate as lifeless and dead.

GRINDING IT

But if the natural packaging of the bean is broken, in other words if the coffee is ground, it will go stale in a few hours. The delicate oils are exposed and immediately begin evaporating. An airtight container will help, but not much. The oxygen and moisture are in there with the broken coffee, destroying the delicate oils, even if you never open the package again.

a useless gesture

Canning coffee is one of those useless gestures typical of convenience foods. Essentially the natural coffee package, the bean, is broken down, and replaced with a can, an inefficient artificial package. Furthermore, canned coffee is not only pre-ground, but *pre-staled.* Freshly roasted and ground coffee releases carbon dioxide gas. If the coffee were put in the cans fresh, the gas could swell the strongest can and turn it into an egg-shaped time bomb. Various technological solutions have been found to this problem, but none strikes me as in any way conducive to richly flavored coffee. And when the consumer does break open the artificial package, he may find a coffee still relatively fresh—but not for long. Since the thousands of small natural packages that make up a pound of coffee have already been broken into, the oxygen that enters the can every time you peel off the plastic lid rapidly completes the job the canning process started.

grind your own

So the easiest and most effective approach is to break down the bean as close as possible to the moment you want to use it; in other words, *grind your coffee just before you brew it.* Grinding your coffee fresh takes very little time. Grinders are inexpensive, and range from quickie electrics to magnificent replicas of old hand grinders. And there is *no one thing that you can do that will increase the quality of your coffee more.*

ideal routine

So the ideal coffee routine for the urban home would be: Buy the coffee whole bean, preferably a half-pound at a time and preferably from a store where they roast it on the spot. Put it in an airtight container in a cool, dark place, and take out only as much as you want to grind and brew immediately. When I say airtight I mean it. No recycled coffee cans or cottage cheese cartons with snap-on plastic lids; rather a solid glass jar with a rubber gasket inside the cap that gives a good seal.

If buying the coffee in half-pound lots isn't practical because you live in the country, then the airtight container and the grinder become even more important. If you do order your coffee by mail and you know about how much coffee you consume by month, you can put in a standing order with a coffee roaster (see section on resources at the back of this book), so your coffee comes fresh every other week, a couple of pounds at a time.

Or better yet buy a large supply of green beans and roast your own. As I indicate in the previous chapter, roasting is simple, and permits you to develop a virtual cellar of exotic coffee beans.

don't freeze

I don't recommend freezing roasted beans, and putting them in the refrigerator is absolutely silly, even in an airtight container. Moisture is the deadly enemy of roasted coffee; the flavor "oils" in roasted coffee are in fact not oils at all, but very delicate, volatile water-soluble substances that moisture immediately dilutes and odors taint. And recall, refrigerators tend to be both damp and smelly. Freezing is better, but even in a good freezer deterioration takes place rather rapidly.

Use an airtight jar in a cool dark place, and if you love coffee and can't shop for it at least every other week, start roasting your own.

BUYING A GRINDER

first choice

There is an awesome number of coffee mills and grinders on the market, even a lot of *kinds* of mills and grinders. I haven't taken them all home and tested them, by any means. I have taken enough of them home to make some solid recommendations. Please, however, don't assume that because I have not recommended an appliance, it is not a good choice. It simply may mean that I haven't had the opportunity to try it. If a coffee grinder comes recommended by a reliable specialty coffee seller and you like the look of it, buy it.

A note on the terms "coffee mill" and "coffee grinder." Currently the industry is attempting to use the two terms to distinguish between, on one hand, appliances that tear the coffee apart by means of corrugated plates or burrs, and on the other, those that knock the coffee apart by means of rap-

GRINDING IT

idly whirling blades. Unfortunately, there is no consensus on which term applies to which set of appliances, and one finds catalogs and retailers flip-flopping the terms according to their own view of the matter. Consequently, I use "grinder" in these pages to describe *all* implements used to reduce coffee beans to brewable proportions. May the most persuasive designation prevail.

Prices indicated are retail by catalog or stores in the San Francisco Bay Area as of January 1987; the first figure indicates the normal retail price; the second figure is the lowest discounted price I was able to turn up.

four ways to grind

Despite the pretensions of modern technology, there are still only four ways to grind coffee. The oldest is the mortar and pestle. The next oldest is the millstone, updated to steel burrs or corrugated plates. The next most recent is the roller mill, which is used only in giant commercial grinders. The most recent is the electric blade grinder, which works on the same principle as the electric blender.

mortar and pestle

If you're *really* into getting back to basics, the mortar and pestle may be the grinder for you. It's cheap, esthetically satisfying, builds up your wrist muscles, and satisfies the profound suspicion so many of us harbor that if it doesn't tire you out it's not really good for you. However, the mortar and pestle does have technical drawbacks: It takes too long, you can't grind much at a time, and it's hard to get an even grind. The price is right, though ($3 to $25).

millstone

Which brings us up through history to the next method, and still the best: Very early in its history coffee was ground between the same millstones that the early peoples of the Middle East used to reduce grains to flour. Later, the Turkish-style coffee grinder was evolved, a small cylinder-shaped implement with a crank on the top that looks and works like a pepper mill. Once the big stones became little corrugated steel plates, this sort of grinder has actually never been improved upon. All sorts of variations have been developed over the years, including hitching the plates to an electric motor, but the principle remains the same. The heart of the grinder is two little corrugated steel disks, or a corrugated steel cone that fits inside a second hollow corrugated cone. One element is stationary and the other is rotated by a handle or motor. The coffee is fed, a bean or two at a time, between the corrugated disks, where it is crushed until it drops out of the bottom of the grinder. This solution has never been beaten because, one, the *grind is uniform,* and two, by adjusting the space between the plates one can regulate the fineness of the grind accurately and consistently.

The cheapest hand grinders are the wooden hand-held models. The beans are fed through a little door in the top of the box, and the ground coffee falls into a little drawer at the bottom. They are adjustable for any except the finest grind. Most look like Van Eyk-period Dutch, but are manufactured everywhere from Japan to Hoboken. Last time I checked, these wooden box-type grinders ranged in price from as little as $10 to as much as $50. To get a hand grinder that really works well, however, you will probably need to pay at least $35 for one of the Zassenhaus line. The Zassenhaus grinders are widely available at specialty coffee stores. They add a clean, northern European look to the romance of the box grinder, are technically excellent, and range in price from about $35 to $45. Italy exports a variety of large, magnificent box grinders, which sell for around $50 when you can find them. The only importer in the San Francisco area recently discontinued handling them, and I can offer no substitute.

box grinders

The problems the box grinder offers are several: With the cheaper versions you can't get a grind fine enough for many coffee brewers, owing to the small and inefficient grinding plates. In even the good ones the crank may be too short for good leverage. Worst of all, the grinder tends to slide around on the table. One of the Zassenhaus designs gets around this problem by introducing a little indentation in facing sides of the grinder, thus permitting you to sit and hold the grinder between your knees as you crank.

problems

Hand grinders that mount on the table or wall solve most of the problems posed by smaller hand-held box grinders. They have longer han-

GRINDING IT

dles, can be screwed down, and usually produce more uniform grinds because the plates are larger. The best currently available is the British Spong hand mill, a wonderful early-industrial-look object ($55/$45). Hand grain mills with metal plates work even better, although they take more space in the kitchen and are hard to find. The best of these, the Polish-made OB grain mill, is no longer available in the United States. With cut-steel plates, at $25 or so, it was a wonderful bargain. One can still order the Colombian Corona Mill ($40/$34) through either Whole Earth Access Company in Berkeley, California, or Paprikas-Weiss in New York City (see Resources). The grinding burrs are tin plated, so I can't give the Corona Mill an unqualified positive recommendation. By the way, do *not* buy a grain mill with stone burrs; the stones get gummy and do not operate well with coffee.

grain mills

On to the 20th century. One type of electric grinder simply powers the same old burrs or steel plates with electricity. The big grinders you see in grocery and coffee stores work on this principle, as do the somewhat smaller grinders you see poking up next to espresso machines in cafés.

There are small household versions of these larger machines made by Krups, Braun, and Bosch, ranging in price from around $45 to $55. You put the beans in a receptacle at the top of the appliance, and ground coffee appears in another receptacle at the bottom. To those who have not lived with these machines, this procedure undoubtedly sounds wonderfully efficient. In practice it is not. These machines require a lot of shaking, fussing, and cleaning, and produce an only slightly more uniform grind than the cheaper blade grinders. If you buy one you will need to do the following: 1) Clean the aperture where the ground coffee spurts out virtually every time you use the grinder; 2) regularly open the grinder to the coarsest setting and run it empty to clear the coffee path; and 3) periodically take the grinder apart completely and clean the insides with a stiff brush. These precautions are particularly important if you grind oily, dark-roasted coffees for espresso.

shaking, fussing,
and cleaning

Hand Grinders
1. Grain Mill
2. Spong

Electric Grinders
3. Burr Type
4. Blade Type

GRINDING IT

The ultimate benefit of the electric burr grinder can only be gotten by spending $100 to $200 on one of the larger machines intended for use with home espresso machines. (See chapter 7.) For the true espresso fanatic, these sturdy, consistent grinders are a necessity. And for the more generalized coffee fanatic, some can function as a general grinder for all brewing needs, depending on the range of grind they permit and the degree of fussiness of the delivery system for the ground coffee. Jericho, an American firm, has introduced a smaller home version of the old-fashioned red-enameled electric store grinder (about $200). Consult a good specialty coffee seller. All of the machines I've tried in this class are strong, well-made appliances.

blade grinders

The third and last development in coffee grinding could only take place in an electrified society. Two steel blades whirr at extremely high speed at the bottom of a cup-like receptacle and literally knock the coffee beans to pieces. With the burr method the fineness of the grind is controlled by the distance between the plates, whereas with the blade method fineness is controlled by the length of time you let the blades whang away at your coffee. This makes the whole process a little hit and miss, unless you're so systematic you start timing yourself.

The disadvantages to the blade grinder? First, like the mortar and pestle, it doesn't make a uniform grind. Some of your coffee will be reduced to a caked-up powder around the edge of the grinder, and some will still be in relatively substantial chunks near the shaft of the blade. I don't think this matters all that much, however, unless you're into Turkish- or Middle Eastern–style coffee, in which case you should simply buy a good hand grinder like the Zassenhaus or Spong, or one of the expensive electric espresso grinders, like the Olympia. Another minor drawback is the difficulty the blade grinder presents in getting the coffee out from under the little blades and into your brewer. You face the same problem when you clean your grinder.

The blade grinder's advantages are more succinctly stated: It is cheap, quick, and it doesn't take up much space in the kitchen. Currently the best is the Bosch ($24), which has low-slung blades close to the bottom of the receptacle, and a receptacle shape that is slanted toward one end, making the job of getting the coffee out of the grinder somewhat easier. All of the many competing blade grinders work well, however, and at this writing are uniformly discounted to the same $15 bargain price tag. I have even seen the mass-marketed Regal as low as $11.

You should be careful not to run your blade grinder continuously for more than a few seconds, since it will begin badly heating the ground coffee. If you make a fine grind, grind in spurts of about five seconds each. It also helps to gently bounce the bottom of the grinder on the counter between spurts to tumble the partly ground coffee back down around the blades.

In general, grind your coffee as fine as you can without clogging the holes or turning your coffee to mud. The finer the grind the more contact there will be between coffee and hot water, and the faster and more thoroughly the essential oils will be released, without further releasing harsher, less soluble chemicals.

On the other hand, you don't want a powder, because by completely pulverizing coffee you again destroy the essential oil; the heat and friction of the grinding process literally vaporizes it. Nor, of course, do you want to clog the holes in your coffee maker or filter or fill your cup with sediment.

Some brewing methods have special requirements. Both Middle Eastern coffee and espresso are special cases, as are open-pot and Melior or plunger-pot coffee. For details, see chapters 6 and 7.

6 BREWING IT
Choosing a method and a machine; brewing it right

NO MATTER what they're called, all ways of brewing coffee are basically the same: You soak the ground coffee in the water until the water tastes good and then you drink it. Nobody to my knowledge has figured out a different way to make coffee. And the only equipment you really need to make great coffee is an open pot, a flame, and possibly a strainer.

It's a tribute to human imagination and lust for perfection, however, that the simple act of combining hot water and ground coffee has produced so many ingenious variations, and occupied so many brilliant people for uncounted hours through the past three centuries. Thousands of coffee makers have been patented in the United States and Europe, but of this multitude only a handful have had any lasting effect or embodied any genuine innovation. The few bright ideas to achieve greatness can be divided according to three variables: how hot one makes the water; how one gets the water to the coffee; and how one separates the spent grounds from the brewed coffee.

three variables

Until the 18th century coffee was almost always boiled. Anyone who has read this far knows boiling damages coffee flavor because it vaporizes much of the coffee essence, while continuing to extract other bitter-tasting

BREWING IT

chemicals. The French began steeping, as opposed to boiling, their coffee in the early years of the 18th century, but this innovation did not penetrate the mainstream of coffee-drinking consciousness until the 19th century, and had to wait until the 20th to triumph. Today, all American and European methods favor hot (around 200°F), as opposed to boiling, water.

water temperature

But if boiling water has been universally nixed, cold water has not. You can steep coffee in cold water and get substantially the same results as with hot water; the only difference is the process takes longer (several hours longer), and makes an extremely mild brew. Since reheating destroys flavor in coffee, cold-water coffee is made concentrated, and mixed with hot water like instant.

getting the water to the coffee

The second variable—how you get the water to your coffee—is a question of convenience. If you're in no hurry and want to hang around the kitchen, you might just as well heat the water in a pot and pour it over the coffee yourself. But if you want to get dressed, make love, or pet the cat while the coffee's brewing, then you might want a way to deliver the hot water to the coffee automatically. Furthermore, coffee making requires consistent and precise timing, a virtue difficult to maintain in our distracted age. The advantage to machines is their single-mindedness; they make coffee the same way every time, even if the phone rings.

The earliest effort at automation was the pumping percolator, originated in 1827 in France, the cradle of coffee-brewing invention. The French subsequently ignored it, but the United States, the cradle of convenience, adopted it enthusiastically. The pumping percolator uses the bubble power of boiling water to force little spurts of hot water up a tube and over the top of the coffee. The hot water, having seeped back through the coffee, returns to the reservoir to mix with the slowly bubbling water at the bottom of the pot. The process continues until the coffee is brewed.

Around 1840, the vacuum principle in coffee brewing was simultaneously discovered by several tinkerers, including a Scots naval engineer, Robert Napier. Napier's original looks more like a steam engine than a coffee maker, but as it has evolved today, the vacuum pot consists of two glass globes which fit tightly together, one above the other, with a cloth filter between. The ground coffee is placed in the upper globe, and water brought to boil in the lower. The two globes are fitted together and the heat lowered. Pressure developed by expanding water vapor in the lower globe forces the water into the upper, where it mixes with the ground coffee. After an interval of one to three minutes, the pot is removed from the heat and the light vacuum formed in the lower globe pulls the brewed coffee back down through the filter.

Finally, the 20th century has brought us both the automatic electric percolator, beloved of wedding guests, and the automatic filter-drip coffee maker, which holds the water in a reservoir above or next to the coffee, heats it, and measures it automatically over the ground coffee either by gravity or by the same bubble power that drives the percolator.

Now we reach the brewing operation which has stimulated coffee-pot tinkerers to their most extravagant efforts: the separation of brewed coffee from spent grounds. Again, original ideas are few, refinements endless. The *separation of brew and grounds* Middle Easterner has the simplest solution: He simply lets most of the grounds settle to the bottom of the cup, and drinks the rest along with the brew. A very direct approach, like everything else about Middle Eastern coffee making. The original coffee drinkers, the Saudi Arabians, grind their beans more coarsely, and strain the coffee into the cup. This of course is a variation of the ubiquitous open-pot method, in which the consumer has the opportunity to invent his own methods for separating grounds from coffee.

The Arabian method was probably the earliest form of coffee brewing, the Middle Eastern or "Turkish" style having been developed later in Egypt. A third development took place in Vienna in 1684, after the lifting of the siege of Vienna, when Franz Georg Kolshitsky opened Central Europe's first cafe with coffee left behind by the routed Turks. Kolshitsky first tried to serve his booty Turkish style, but the Viennese wouldn't go for it. They called it "stewed soot," and continued to drink white wine and lager beer for

BREWING IT

breakfast. But when Kolshitsky started straining his coffee and serving it with milk and honey his success was assured; within a few years Vienna's great café tradition was well established. Strained or separated coffee has dominated European and American taste ever since.

the world's *favorite*

An 18th-century Frenchman named De Belloy is credited with discovering the world's favorite method of separating coffee from grounds: the drip pot. Hot water is poured into an upper compartment with the coffee, and allowed to drip through a strainer or filter into a lower compartment, leaving the coffee grounds behind. An impressive variety of refinements has been developed since, including the Neapolitan flip pot, the cloth filter, and disposable paper filters.

One other method of separation deserves mention: After the coffee is steeped, a metal filter or strainer is forced *down through* the coffee like a plunger, squashing the coffee grounds to the bottom of the pot and leaving the clarified coffee above. There is no accepted generic name for this sort of brewer; we could call it a "plunger pot" which I like, or "French press," after the country of origin.

GENERAL CONSIDERATIONS *in buying a brewer*

Your pot ideally should be made of glass or porcelain. Stainless steel will do. But if you have a choice in the matter, avoid aluminum. Food cooked in aluminum absorbs minute traces of the metal; coffee held for long in aluminum will develop a metallic flatness. When one adds to the danger to flavor the tendency of aluminum to pit and corrode, I think there is ample reason to avoid the metal in your coffee maker. Tin plate may also faintly taint coffee.

Your pot should be easy to clean. Coffee is oily, and allowed to accumulate this oil will eventually contribute a stale taste to fresh coffee. Stubborn brown stains in the corners can be soaked out with a strong solution of baking soda or one of the commercial urn cleaners on the market. Glass and porcelain are easiest to clean; aluminum and tin-coated metal the hardest. It is wise to avoid pots with seams or cracks, especially in the part which comes in direct contact with the brewed coffee. You might also check to make sure you can take the whole thing apart easily for an occasional thorough cleaning. In areas with alkaline, or hard water, a lime deposit will build up even in the parts of your maker which are untouched by coffee. The universal remedy is a strong solution of vinegar. Run it through the works of your brewer, and rinse thoroughly.

And now for the inevitable list of brewing rules and precepts. No matter whose invention you use to brew your coffee, I urge you to:

BREWING
SUGGESTIONS

- Use fresh coffee. Grind it as close to the moment you brew it as possible.
- Grind it as fine as you can make it without losing any through the holes in your coffee maker's filter, but never to an absolute powder. French press, conventional (non-filter) drip, and open-pot brewing require a less fine grind.
- Use plenty of coffee: at least two level tablespoons or one standard "coffee measure" per five- to six-ounce cup. You may want to use more, but I strongly suggest you never use less. Most mugs hold closer to eight ounces than six, so if you measure by the mug use two and a half to three level tablespoons for every mug of water. Coffee brewed strongly tastes better, and you can enjoy the distinction in your favorite coffee more clearly. If you brew with hard water or if you drink your coffee with milk, you should be especially careful to brew strong. If you feel that you're sensitive to caffeine, cut your coffee with caffeine-free beans (Chapter 9).
- Keep your coffee maker clean, and rinse it with hot water before you brew.
- Use fresh water, as free of impurities and alkalines as possible.

BREWING IT

● Brew with hot water, as opposed to lukewarm or boiling (Middle Eastern and cold-water coffee are exceptions). A temperature of 200°F is ideal, which means bringing the water to boil and waiting a couple of minutes before brewing. If you've done everything else right and you're in a rush, however, water that has just stopped boiling certainly won't overly hurt a good, freshly ground coffee.

● In filter and drip systems avoid brewing less than your brewer's full capacity: If the pot is made to brew six cups, your coffee will taste better if you brew the full six.

● Some don'ts: Don't boil coffee; it cooks off all the delicate flavoring essence, and leaves the bitter chemicals. Don't perk or reheat coffee; it has the same effect as boiling, only less so. Don't hold coffee for very long on the heat; same story. Don't mix old coffee with new; like using rotten wood to prop up a new building.

water quality Ninety-nine percent of a cup of coffee is water, and if you use bad, really bad, water, you might just as well throw away this book and buy a bottle of instant. The simple rule of thumb is this: If the water isn't pleasant to drink, don't make coffee with it. Use bottled or purified water. "Hard," or alkaline water will not directly harm flavor and aroma, but will mute some of the natural acids in coffee, and produce a blander cup without acidy snap. Water which has been treated with softeners makes even worse coffee, however, so if you do live in a hard water area you might either compensate by buying more acidy coffees (African, Arabian, and the best Indonesian and Central American growths), or again, brew with bottled water.

The simplest brewing method is as good as any: You steep the ground coffee in a pot of hot water, strain or otherwise separate the grounds from the brewed coffee, and serve. Open-pot coffee is a favorite of kinky individualists, hermits, hoboes, writers, artists, and other perennially light travelers. I have a sculptor friend who insists on making his in a pot improvised from a coffee can and a coat hanger. For such nonconformists, the real challenge is separating the grounds from the coffee without stooping to the aid of decadent bourgeois inventions like strainers.

OPEN POT

Bring the cold water to a boil and let it cool for a minute or so. Toss in the coffee. Use a moderately fine grind, about what the stores call "drip." Stir gently to break up the lumps and let the mixture steep, covered, for two to four minutes. If you are willing to compromise, obtain a very fine mesh strainer; the best is made of nylon cloth. Strain the coffee and serve. If you consider yourself too authentic for a strainer, pour a couple of spoons of cold water over the surface of the coffee to sink whatever grounds have not already settled; in theory at least the cold water, which is heavier than the hot, will carry these stubbornly buoyant pieces with it to the bottom. If you wish to further clarify your coffee, put the shell of one egg into the pot with the coffee. The shell absorbs some of the sediment which clouds the brew.

For the lazy or less macho, specialty stores sell a little nylon bag ($3 to $5) that sits inside the traditional straight-sided coffee pot, supported on the outside by a plastic ring. These devices have the added advantage of permitting a much finer grind of coffee than the traditional open-pot methods. You put the ground coffee in the nylon bag and pour hot water over it. In two to four minutes you simply lift the bag and grounds out of the brewed coffee.

This is essentially open-pot coffee with a sexy method for separating the grounds from the brew. The pot is a narrow glass cylinder. A fine-meshed screen plunger fits tightly inside the cylinder; you put a fine-ground coffee in the cylinder, pour boiling water over it, and insert the plunger in

FRENCH PRESS
plunger

BREWING IT

the top of the cylinder without pushing it down. After about four minutes the coffee will be thoroughly steeped and you push the plunger down through the coffee, clarifying it and forcing the grounds to the bottom of the pot. You serve the coffee directly from the cylinder. Be certain not to use too fine a grind unless you have an athlete or a weight-lifter at the table; the plunger will become almost impossible to push down through the

straight down coffee. Also be careful to push the plunger *straight* down; if you push from an angle you're liable to break the pot.

The growing popularity of this brewing method has unleashed a flood of French-press brewers, most of them imposters from everywhere except France. One's first decision in purchasing such a brewer is whether to spend a little money on a version that contains the glass brewing receptacle in a plastic frame, or spend a good deal more on a brewer that contains the glass in a metal frame. The plastic frame brewers are generally bright, contemporary looking, and cheap (around $20). I like the looks of the Coffee Presso imported by Bodum, with its angular frame flared at the base. The traditional metal-framed French silhouette brewers are produced in France (the original Melior Chambord, $100 to $120), in China ($40 to $70), and in Japan (Hario, imported by Jericho America, $40 to $100).

There are subtle differences in manufacture and design both within and among these product lines. The frames range from nickle plate to chrome-plated brass to chrome-plated steel. More important is the quality of the glass brewing decanter: Check for air bubbles and lines in the glass before purchasing. Finally, a stainless mesh filter is superior to a nylon mesh filter, and a metal plunger knob to a plastic knob. My personal favorite is the Alessi (three-cup $80, eight-cup $95), with a sturdy, slotted metal frame that manages to look contemporary and traditional at the same time.

Both open-pot and plunger-style coffee tend to be rich in sediment, oils, and minute globs of gelatinous stuff that neither settle nor dissolve, which chemists call colloids. Coffee made by the filter method has far less of this stuff; filter coffee brewed by the cold-water method has least of all. Some people prefer their coffee as clear and free from such minute muck as possible; such purists should choose a filter brewer. But for those of us who like the heavier body and richer, more idiosyncratic flavor of coffee *with* the muck, open-pot or French-press brewing is a good choice.

more idiosyncratic

The question of muck aside, advantages of the French press are its value as a conversation piece, its portability (you can brew coffee at the table rather than messing around with filters and such in the kitchen), and its elegance, all of which make it an ideal after-dinner brewer. The plunger pot is, however, a bit harder to clean than most drip or filter pots.

The drip pot was invented by a Frenchman around 1800 and popularized by Count Rumford, an eccentric American who became a Count of the Holy Roman Empire, married two rich widows, the second one French, and spent much of his leisure time making enemies and coffee. The drip maker typically consists of two compartments, an upper and lower, divided by a metal or ceramic "filter," or strainer. The ground coffee is placed in the upper compartment and hot water poured over it. The brewed coffee trickles through the strainer into the lower compartment.

DRIP

A very attractive porcelain drip pot, with an elegant, traditionally French silhouette, can be bought at specialty stores for anywhere from $30 to $50. The French also make individual one-cup drip coffee makers which fit over the cup. You fill the top with hot water and the coffee drips directly into the cup.

A popular variation of the drip pot was invented in 1819 by Marize, a French tinsmith. This is the reversible, double, or flip-drip pot, which has since been adopted by the Italians as the "Neapolitan" pot. Rather than being laid loosely on top of the strainer, as in the regular drip pot, the

Neapolitan flip-drip

1. French Press
2. French Drip
3. Neapolitan Flip-Drip

1.

2.

3.

ground coffee is secured in a two-sided strainer at the waist of the pot. The water is heated in one side of the pot, then the whole thing is flipped over, and the hot water drips through the coffee into the other, empty side. There are several versions of the Neapolitan machinetta, or flip-drip pot, available. An aluminum version is the cheapest—around $8 for the smallest, up to $10 for the largest. Since aluminum is not a desirable material for coffee brewers, I recommend instead one of the several attractive copper versions at around $30, or a modern-look stainless, also at $30.

Use as fine a grind of coffee as possible in your drip brewer. If the coffee drips through painfully slowly or not at all, or if you find more sediment in your cup than you prefer, try a coarser grind. Even with the correct grind you may find that you will need to give your pot an occasional little tap or jostle to keep the coffee dripping through. When you pour the hot water over the ground coffee, make certain that you saturate *all* of the coffee, to prevent dry lumps from islanding up and getting left out of the brewing process. Cover to preserve heat. Mix the coffee lightly after it has brewed, since the first coffee to drip through is stronger and heavier than the last. Both drip and filter coffees often cool excessively during the brewing process; it helps to preheat the bottom half of the pot with hot tap water before brewing. If that isn't enough, buy a heat-reducing pad and keep your pot on the stove while you're brewing. If you're troubled by sediment, disposable cloth filters are available to fit most drip brewers.

*saturate
all the grounds*

Until recently, the pop of a pumping percolator at work producing coffee ranked along with the acceleration of a well-tuned car as one of North America's best-loved sounds. However, the pumping percolator is probably the one brewing device you will *not* find in your neighborhood specialty store. However reassuring the sensuous gurgle of a percolator is psychologically, chemically it means only one thing: You're boiling your coffee, and prematurely vaporizing the delicate flavoring oils. Every pop of the

PERCOLATOR

percolator means another bubble of aroma and flavor is bursting at the top of the pot, bestowing its gift on your kitchen rather than on your palate.

Opinions differ as to the extent of the damage the percolator inflicts on coffee flavor. *Consumer Reports* magazine (September 1974) served coded cups of drip and percolator coffee both to "experts" and to its staff. The experts unanimously and consistently preferred the drip coffee to the perked coffee, but the staff's reaction was mixed. I find I can invariably pick out perked coffee in a similar test by the slightness of its aroma and a flat, slightly bitter edge to the flavor. Certainly, however, there are more ways to ruin coffee than to put it in a good pumping percolator; really stale coffee, for instance, tastes bad no matter how you brew it. A fresh canned coffee brewed with care in a good pumping percolator certainly tastes better than mishandled, three-month-old Jamaican Blue Mountain.

If you must have a pumping percolator, a good electric is probably the best choice, since the heat is automatically controlled to produce a perk rather than a boil, and most electrics have a thermostat that should reduce the heat at the optimum moment to prevent overextraction.

VACUUM

Coffee made by the vacuum-filter method does not differ markedly from coffee made with other filter systems. Since the manipulations involved are a bit more complex than those demanded by the filter method, the vacuum pot has lost considerable popularity since its heyday in the twenties and thirties. But for some the leisurely and alchemical shifting of liquids in the two glass globes has a continuing appeal, and the coffee produced should be as good as any. In fact, some cultures that value ceremony are particularly fond of the vacuum filter. In Japan, for instance, one-cup vacuum brewers are universally used in coffee houses to custom brew specialty "call" coffees. Unfortunately, the charm of the gesture considerably transcends the quality of the coffee; everywhere I went in Japan the flame was kept so dramatically high under the brewer that the coffee was essentially boiled, losing most of its distinction and subtlety in the process.

1.

2.

1. Automatic Filter Drip
2. Cona Vacuum

BREWING IT

Which proves, I suppose, that one does need patience to make good vacuum-filter coffee. At this writing the only vacuum brewer I could find generally available in the United States was the simple and attractive six-cup Bodum ($20), a stove-top model. For those who wish to brew at the table, the Bodum comes with a simple but attractive stand and spirit lamp for around $60 the set. The wonderfully esoteric British Cona Table Model ($90 to $100) and French Hellem ($90 to $120) brew coffee by means of a spirit lamp only, and are obviously meant to be brought out after dinner for leisurely at-the-table ceremony. After several minutes of exquisitely complex maneuvers, they will produce two or three cups of excellent coffee brewed by impeccable filter principles. Unfortunately, neither appears to be imported generally to the United States any longer, although there may be a few dusty specimens still waiting in specialty stores for the enthusiast.

leisurely ceremony

FILTER

Coffee-pot tinkerers started using cloth filters around 1800; disposable paper filters came later, and were never really popular until after World War II. The main objection to paper filters then and now: They must be continually replaced. The main objection to cloth filters: They get dirty and are difficult to clean. In our disposable age the paper filter has triumphed, but permanent filters, in the form of nylon mesh or gold-plated metal, are currently making inroads. The use of these devices blurs the distinction between ordinary drip brewing and filter brewing, since they essentially turn a filter brewer into a drip brewer. The description and admonitions that follow refer to coffee brewed with disposable paper filters, not with metal or nylon mesh filters.

Nearly all filter coffee makers work the same way. A paper filter is placed in a plastic, glass, or ceramic holder; fine-ground (a fine grit just short of powdery) coffee goes in the filter, and the filter container goes atop a flameproof glass or ceramic flask. From there you proceed as you do for drip coffee (see page 103).

BREWING IT

The advantages of filter brewing: It permits you to use a very fine grind of coffee and effect a quick and thorough extraction, and the paper filters make grounds easy to dispose of and your coffee maker easy to keep clean. Because of their simplicity and popularity, coffee cones are the cheapest coffee brewing devices on the market. Those who like a light-bodied clear coffee free of oils, colloids, and sediment will enjoy a good filter coffee; those who like a heavier, richer brew will prefer other methods.

advantages

The disadvantages: Paper filters slow the drip process to such a degree that the coffee may require warming before drinking. And, though your initial investment in the cone may be small, you'll be paying for filters for the rest of your coffee-drinking career. The first of these disadvantages can be circumvented: Lukewarm coffee can be avoided by keeping your pot over low heat buffered by a heat-reducing device or a hot water bath, or on an electric warmer. The expense of paper filters can be avoided by purchasing a reuseable cloth filter available in specialty stores for about $3, but I don't recommend these compromise filters; they take too much out of the coffee and are hard to keep clean. I might add that filter coffee tastes best when brewed in large quantities; the big restaurant urns that take a pound of ground coffee at a time brew splendid coffee; an eight-cup filter brewer will make very good coffee; a one-cup filter cone tends to make a weak, mediocre cup no matter what you do. This phenomenon of diminishing return in proportion to diminishing filter brewer size is well known in the coffee trade; what causes it I'm not certain, but I suspect it has something to do with the relatively greater proportion of filter paper surface to ground coffee in the smaller brewers. The filter paper simply seems to dominate the coffee in a one-cup cone, filtering out too many of the flavorful oils along with the sediment.

disadvantage

more the better

A last point, which needs to be said carefully: If one runs hot water through most filter papers and tastes the hot water afterwards, the sensitive palate will detect a faint "papery" taste. Whatever produces this taste is without a doubt harmless to health, and could hardly harm the flavor of a

"papery"

robust cup of coffee. As a matter of fact, I can't imagine it adversely affecting the taste of even the most lackluster, insipid cup of coffee. But the taste is there, and if you're the kind of person who insists on feeling peas under mattresses, you may want to make the taste test described above and decide whether you care to switch to another brewing method.

There is an enormous array of filter brewers on the market. One has a choice of material (as always, glass and ceramic are the best) and of filter shape, which runs from the simple cone, to the Melitta-style pocket or wedge, to the flat-bottomed basket filters. Adherents (and manufacturers) of each style make cogent arguments for the technical superiority of their chosen shape. I have not, however, found much difference among coffees made with the three styles of filter. Other factors, such as coffee quality, water quality, water temperature, filter quality, and the care taken in delivering the water to the coffee, appear to be more important than filter shape.

cone-shaped   Among brewers using the cone-shaped filters, the most famous is the Chemex, the original American filter brewer that was developed from, and still resembles, a well-made piece of laboratory equipment. Many will find its austere design (honored by the Museum of Modern Art) and authentic materials (glass and wood in the traditional models) attractive, but the single-piece hourglass shape makes cleaning difficult. The original hand-blown models with wood handles range in price from $40 to $50 depending on capacity; the same models in machine-molded glass run from around $16 to $30. Chemex now also makes a version with an attractive integral glass handle for $22 to $30. If you choose not to set your Chemex in a pot of water or on a stovetop diffusion pad to keep it warm while brewing, you may want to purchase the matching electric warmer ($25). You will definitely need a sturdy bottle brush for cleaning; Chemex makes its own at around $8.

wedge-shaped   The Melitta company, originator of the wedge-shaped pocket filter, is without a doubt the leading producer of filters and filter accessories, both in terms of sales volume and value for the dollar. Melitta products are consistently well made, well designed, and sensibly priced. The top of their line of pour-over coffee makers is a pair of porcelain models; one style is swellingly reminiscent of the traditional French drip silhouette, the other is a contemporary cone-cylinder design (both around $20). Versions with flameproof glass decanter and plastic cone are even cheaper. The contemporary rendition is so elegantly simple that it defies design category (six-cup $14/$12, eight-cup $19/$16). There is also a fatter, browner version with a Howard Johnson-style frieze around the middle ($7 to $11). The only Melitta electric warmer I've recently seen shares the Howard Johnson-style detailing of the low-end brewer, but is a bargain (around $13).

The latest thing in heat preservation for drip coffee is the thermos brewer. A filter cone sits on top of a thermos; you filter your coffee directly into the preheated thermos, and the heat-loss problem endemic to filter systems is solved. There are many on the market ($17 to $25); if you already have a thermos, Melitta probably makes a filter unit to fit it.

A note on permanent filters. I don't recommend cloth filters, since *permanent* they are difficult to keep clean. The Rittergold gold-plated permanent fil- *filters* ters, in both standard Melitta wedge and basket styles, seem to be all the rage these days. They are an excellent product, but if you really like filter coffee, you will not like coffee made with these filters as well as coffee brewed with paper filters. The Rittergold or any similar mesh filter allows a good deal of sediment and colloids to enter the brewed coffee, which gives it a heavier, often gritty taste, closer in style to drip or French-plunger coffee. These permanent filters also require a coarser and more uniform grind to work correctly.

Careful brewing can make a considerable difference in the quality of filter coffee. Bring cold water to just short of boiling and pour just a little over the grounds, making sure all the coffee gets wet. Pour the rest of the water through, and stir the coffee lightly after brewing. If you make a small quantity, less than four cups, you should use slightly more ground coffee to compensate for the flavor lost to the filter.

BREWING IT

AUTOMATIC
FILTER DRIP

The latest thing in the coffee world. In 1973, some automatic-filter-drip coffee makers were sold in the United States. In 1974, that figure rose to three million, and doubled to six million in 1975. Today, the automatic filter drip has virtually eliminated the electric percolator from the market in larger cities. Either America is in love with a new gimmick, or the American coffee drinker always did consider filter coffee better, but clung to the percolator because it saved time and steps.

The heart of the automatic-filter-drip system is the familiar filter, receptacle, and decanter. The machine simply heats water to the optimum heat for coffee brewing and automatically measures it into the filter. The coffee drips into the decanter, and an element under the decanter keeps the coffee hot once it is brewed. The consumer measures cold water into the top of the maker, measures coffee into the filter, presses a switch, and in from four to eight minutes has four to 12 cups of coffee.

improved performance

Furthermore, the manufacturers of these brewers have improved performance over the past several years. In 1980, a *Consumer Reports* article rated coffee brewed by only one of 23 automatic drip machines tested as "totally satisfactory." I don't think that woeful performance would be duplicated today. Most of the leading makers have resolved problems like ground coffee floating or "donuting" up around the edges of the filter basket, variations in water temperature, and excessively slow or fast filtering.

Nevertheless, I find that even the best of these brewers do not make coffee as well as I can make it by simply pouring the water over the ground coffee by hand. But the best machines come close, and most of the really egregiously bad performers appear to have been eliminated from the shelves.

high end

On the high end of the price-positioning scale are the Eurostyled brewers by Krups, Braun, and Melitta; for a plain model without clocks and gimmicks these machines will run from about $35 to close to $75. These makers tend to be in white or "designer" colors, and are sleek, authoritative, and reticent in profile. They appear primarily on the shelves of large, upscale department stores and coffee specialty stores, although at this writing Braun seemed to be making a run on the mass market by aggressively marketing its basic 12-cup maker through discount drug stores and suburban shopping-mall chains.

On the low end, there are the mass-marketed, entry-level brewers by makers like Proctor-Silex, Regal, and Hamilton Beach; these machines run to browns and wood grains, are squarish in styling and ingratiatingly obvious in their workings; i.e., you usually can see the coffee dribble into the carafe. There has been a recent price breakthrough with some of these brewers; several list for as little as $20, and at this writing can be purchased discounted with rebate for $10.

low end

As would be expected with an aggressively marketed appliance designed for convenience and saving time, there is an insistent chorus of features that add to the price of the fundamental entry-level brewer, as found in your local discount department store. You can get:

chorus of features

- A "pause" feature that enables you to temporarily interrupt the brewing cycle to obtain an immediate cup.
- Under-the-counter design, enabling you to save space. Obviously only you and your kitchen can decide on the usefulness of this feature.
- A thermos carafe, designed to keep the coffee hot without the usual warming plate. Useful for those who hold coffee for any length of time: A sealed thermos retains flavor and some aroma, whereas both tend to deteriorate rapidly when the coffee is subjected to an external heat source like a hot plate. Naturally, the best solution for the enthusiast is to buy a smaller-capacity brewer and brew more often.
- A closed system, designed to retain heat and aroma during the brewing process. This feature accounts for the reticent look of the high-end brewers. Nearly all of the recently redesigned brewers incorporate a closed system in one way or another, and the de-

signer brewers, like Krups and Braun, make a very strong case for this feature in their promotional materials. If all else is equal, a closed system undoubtedly improves flavor and aroma. However, if you let your coffee sit on the hot plate for fifteen minutes before you drink it, a feature like this is rendered automatically irrelevant.

clocks • Clocks that enable you to set your brewer to wake you up with freshly brewed coffee. You fill the water and coffee receptacles the night before and set the timer. The advantage is obvious. The disadvantage is the ground coffee stales all night long. Still, I wouldn't hold it against any coffee lover who bought one. In its My Cafe model, Toshiba tries to eliminate the staling issue by building in a grinder that also automatically *grinds* the coffee in the morning before brewing. But no, it does *not* go to the store to buy the coffee for you.

permanent filters • Permanent filters of nylon or metal mesh. If you like the clarity and brightness of filtered coffee, you will probably find this feature useless. Certainly avoid buying a maker that *only* permits you to use the permanent filter, and does not give you the option of using paper.

• Coffee-strength controls. Those that I've tried are useless; the "strong" setting causes the coffee to be overbrewed and consequently harsh.

• A provision for brewing smaller amounts of coffee. This feature on the latest Krups machines actually appears to work. In the case of most other machines, it simply involves a smaller basket for the ground coffee.

Beware of funny-shaped decanters that are difficult to clean, and brewers that need to be unplugged to turn them off. There are also invisible defects: brewers that take far too long to heat water and brew, and one or two whose hot plates virtually boil the coffee. The only way to avoid these problems is to buy one of my recommended brewers or check the latest *Consumer Reports* or other buyer's guide. As I indicated earlier, most of these real losers are redesigned or off the market.

My recommendations are necessarily sketchy, since 60 or 70 models are presently on the market, and more appear every month. Please don't assume my failing to mention a brewer implies condemnation.

recommendations

High-End Recommendations At $40 to $120, these are the designer coffee makers, Eurostyled, marketed primarily through department stores and specialty coffee stores:

All-Around Best (and Most Expensive) Krups Aroma Master ($95/$60). This latest Krups appears to have no faults and all of the useful features I list above except the under-the-counter styling and the thermos carafe. The version with digital timer goes for a stiff $150/$100. All models are very good looking, and have many small, thoughtfully considered design details. They make as good a cup of filter coffee as is made currently by any machine marketed, and consistently come out on top in various consumer magazine and consumer institute tastings.

Best Value The Melitta "SCM" line of automatic drip brewers: more compact than the Krups, not quite as sleek, but with the same range of features at lower prices ($50/$40 for full-featured 10-cup, $70/$50 with timer). For some reason Melitta was not included in the latest *Consumer Reports* tests, but I find that these newest models make an excellent cup of coffee.

Best Looking The reticent and sleek Braun line offers the same range of features as the Krups and Melitta, with the addition of a version with thermos carafe ($75/$60). At this writing, Braun brewers are being aggressively priced to compete with the Melitta line and even with traditionally lower-priced brewers like the Norelco series. The Braun brewers make excellent coffee, but draw persistent criticism for brewing too slowly, and for maintaining coffee temperature too low for North American tastes.

Low-End Recommendations At $10 to $40, these are the plain-folks brewers marketed primarily through discount department stores, oversized drug stores, and so forth.

Poor Man's Designer Brewer Norelco puts out an excellent line of brewers with some of the features of the high-end machines; their low-end 10-cup Norelco Ready Brew at $40/$25 has a fussy, useless brew-strength control, but makes an excellent cup of coffee; the real bargain is a 10-cup with analog timer at $47/$40.

Best Buy The Proctor-Silex 10-cup brewer has no fancy features whatsoever, but in my experience makes a good, consistent cup of coffee, and the price is unbeatable (mass-marketed through discount department stores and drug stores at around $20, with rebate as low as $10). Also look for the West Bend brewers in about the same price range.

out on a limb   If I were to go out on a limb on all this, I would recommend that you buy a $12 Melitta cone-and-decanter set, pour the water over the coffee yourself and forget about these plastic robots. But if convenience counts for you, at least shop for a good brewer, and grind your coffee as fine as possible within the manufacturer's suggested limits in order to obtain the maximum extraction.

The Toshiba My Cafe, noted earlier, is in a category all its own (eight-cup $120/$65; 12-cup $175/$130). It is an anomaly in two respects: It does not take paper filters, making it an automatic drip rather than automatic filter drip, and, more spectacularly, it grinds and brews coffee in the same receptacle. You measure whole coffee beans into the brewing basket, lock on a cover, and set a digital timer. At the appointed time, a pair of blades knocks apart the coffee, and hot water bubbles over the ground coffee and drips through a stainless-steel filter into the decanter. Grinding and brewing both happen in the same basket receptacle.

All coffee made with a mesh (rather than paper) filter will be rich in sediment and oils. Don't expect coffee from My Cafe to have the bright, clear flavor of good paper-filtered coffee. In fact, I find the My Cafe brewer makes a particularly heavy, silty cup, probably because all blade grinders produce a dusty, uneven grind when they are not manipulated to keep the coffee circulated around the blades. Still, My Cafe is an entertaining gadget, which actually might be useful to someone who likes a heavier style of coffee.

BREWING FOR ONE
(or two)

With the exception of espresso, most brewing systems produce their best coffee in fairly large quantities. I have tried several one-cup brewing systems, and find them all lacking in one way or another.

The flavor loss is particularly acute with filter coffee, since in a one-cup brewer the paper filter overpowers the coffee. So if you are a filter-coffee drinker and after quality, you have little choice but to use a full-sized brewer and brew somewhat more than you need. On the other hand, if you don't mind a little European style grit and oil in your cup, I suggest the Rittergold one-cup metal-mesh filter ($8), which works well for solo brewing, provided you preheat the cup and filter before you brew.

There are several solo electric coffee-making systems on the market, all designed to be portable. The Melitta ($50/$42) is bulky and uses paper filters; although it is manufactured with the usual Melitta quality, I don't recommend it because of the dominating effect of the filter on the coffee. The Ronde Quick Cafe uses a permanent nylon-mesh filter system, is compact and ingeniously designed, and makes an excellent cup of drip-style coffee. The fussy little filters may be too flimsy over the long haul, however. The attractive Maxim ($40) and the rather frumpy Norleco ($30) are two-cup, pour-it-over-yourself travel kits, using permanent metal filters.

BREWING IT

In Latin America as well as in many other parts of the world, a very strong concentrated coffee is brewed, stored, and added in small amounts to hot water or milk to make a sort of pre-industrial instant. It is possible to obtain a strong concentrate with almost any brewing method, although only one, the cold-water method, has obtained much popularity in the United States. To make a hot-water concentrate, use eight cups of water to a pound of finely ground coffee and brew in your customary fashion. If your coffee maker won't handle a pound at a time, halve the recipe or brew twice. Store the resulting concentrate in a stoppered bottle in the refrigerator, and in a preheated cup, add about one ounce to every five ounces of hot water. A shot glass holds an ounce, and makes a convenient measure.

cold-water method

The cold-water concentrate method has been adopted by two manufacturers, Filtron and Toddy. Both make an excellent cold-water brewer for around $18. Both work substantially the same way: You steep a pound of regular-grind coffee in eight cups of cold water for anywhere from 10 to 20 hours, filter the resulting concentrate into a separate container, store it in the refrigerator, and add it, an ounce to a cup, to hot water.

The result is a very mild, delicate brew, with little acidity (of either good or bad variety), light body, a natural sweetness, and an evanescent, muted flavor. Someone who takes his coffee weak and black, and likes a delicate flavor free of acid highlights and the rest of the idiosyncracies of coffee flavor, may well like the cold-water method. Those who for medical reasons require a milder brew also might find it suitable. And it is, like the hot concentrate, convenient.

But anyone who likes strong coffee, distinctive coffee, or coffee with milk would be better off doing it another way. Another problem: If you combine an ounce or more of refrigerated concentrate with five ounces of hot water, you end with a mixture a little less than scalding hot; add milk and your coffee is virtually lukewarm.

Some people like to use cold-water concentrate in cooking, but I prefer a hot-water concentrate because the coffee flavor is stronger and more distinctive; cold-water concentrate makes everything taste like store-bought coffee ice cream. The same can be said for using cold-water concentrate in cold coffee drinks; one needs a concentrate for cold drinks to compensate for ice dilution, but some (like me) prefer the more distinctive punch of hot-brewed concentrate.

You don't have to buy a cold-water brewer to enjoy cold-water coffee, although the store-bought brewers are much more convenient than any expedient. To improvise you need a glass bowl, a large coffee cone and filter, and a bottle with an airtight closure (snap-on plastic won't do) in which to refrigerate the finished concentrate. Take a pound of your favorite coffee, regular grind. You can use any coffee, any roast. Chuck it in the bowl, and add eight cups of cold water. Poke the floating coffee down into the water so all the grounds are wet; then let the bowl stand in a cool, dark corner for anywhere from 10 to 20 hours, depending on how strong you want your concentrate. When the brewing period is over, use your cone to filter the concentrate into the second, airtight container, and store in the refrigerator. For hot coffee, use one to two ounces per cup.

improvising a brewer

Any concentrate will keep its flavor for months if the bottle is tightly capped, but your best bet is to make only as much as you will drink in a

Middle Eastern Coffee Implements

grinder

Ibrik

week or two. The cold water Toddy people say you can freeze the concentrate, but I've found it loses some much-needed flavor, and I suggest you simply halve the recipe if you can't drink a pound's worth in two weeks.

MIDDLE EASTERN
Turkish, Greek

Middle Eastern coffee is most often called "Turkish" coffee in this country, but this is a misnomer. For one thing, it is drunk all over the Middle East, not only in Turkey, and if a patriotic Greek or Armenian serves it to you, you had better *not* call it Turkish coffee. Secondly, according to all accounts the method was invented in Cairo and later spread from there to Turkey and Istanbul. Middle Eastern coffee is unique, first, because some of the coffee grounds are deliberately drunk along with the coffee, and second, because the coffee is usually brewed *with* sugar, rather than sweetened after brewing. Tiny grains of coffee float suspended in the sweetened liquid, imparting a heavy, almost syrupy weight to the cup.

It's possible to make good, flavorful Middle Eastern–style coffee in any old pot; the investment you make in brewing equipment is more important to ritual and esthetics than flavor. But, as I find myself pointing out so often, ritual seems to be as important as flavor in the life of coffee. So if you want to be authentic you'll need one of those small, conical pots (it looks a little like an inverted megaphone) called an *ibrik* (Turkish) or *briki* (Greek). *ibrik* The best and most authentic are made of copper or brass and tinned inside, and cost anywhere from $10 to $20. You should also have demitasse cups and saucers; the standard restaurant variety of brown or plain white porcelain is fine, and can be bought at any large restaurant-supply store.

The most important piece of functional equipment in making Middle Eastern–style coffee is the grinder. Since you drink the grounds, and you *grinder* don't want to be picking grains of coffee from between your teeth, you need a very fine, uniform grind, a dusty powder in fact. Few home mills will produce such a grind. The Corona grain mill and the Zassenhaus box mills described in Chapter 5 will do a fairly decent job. The only electric machines I know of which will produce a consistently good Middle Eastern–style coffee are some of the high-priced specialty espresso grinders, notably the Olympia (see Chapter 2).

Of course there are preground Middle Eastern coffees available, both in cans and prewrapped at your specialty coffee store. Few specialty stores can grind true Middle Eastern coffee for you fresh, by the way; their grinders do not as a rule adjust that fine. They have it preground, which puts it about in the same class as canned coffees.

The roast you choose is a matter of taste, as is the provenance of the coffee. Most "Turkish" or Middle Eastern–style coffee sold in the States is a fairly dark roast, the sort most stores sell as Italian. A blend of a winey

BREWING IT

coffee like Kenya or Mocha, some Sumatran, and a good dark French roast makes an excellent Middle Eastern coffee.

kaimaki

Authentic Middle Eastern coffee should have a thin head of brown foam completely covering the surface of the coffee. In Greece, this is called the *kaimaki,* and to serve coffee without it is an insult to the guest and a disgrace to the host. A Greek friend of mine tells about her mother secretly struggling in their kitchen to produce a good head of *kaimaki,* while the rest of the family nervously diverted the guests with small talk in the parlor. In America, the *kaimaki* is usually dispensed with, for the simple reason that it's very difficult to produce. Your Middle Eastern coffee should taste good the first time you make it, and the foam can wait until you're an expert.

sweetening

Never plan to fill the *ibrik* to more than one-half its capacity. You need the other half to accommodate the foam which will boil up from the coffee. Start by measuring two level-to-rounded teaspoons of freshly ground, powdered coffee per demitasse into the *ibrik.* Add about one level teaspoon of sugar for every teaspoon of coffee. This makes a coffee a Greek would call "sweet"; add one and a half teaspoons of sugar per teaspoon of coffee and you get "heavy sweet"; a half teaspoon is "light sweet"; add no sugar and you're serving your coffee plain, or *sketo.*

brewing

Now measure the water into the *ibrik.* Stir to dissolve the sugar, then turn on the heat, medium to high. After a while the coffee will begin to gently boil. Let it, but watch it closely. Eventually the foam, which should have a darkish crust on top, will begin to climb the narrowing part of the *ibrik.* When it fills the flare at the top of the pot and is at the point of boiling over, turn off the flame. Immediately, and gently, so as not to settle the foam, pour into the cups. Fill each cup halfway first, then return to add some foam to each. Again, even though you may fail with the foam, the coffee will always be delicious.

Middle Easterners like to add all sorts of spices to their coffee. The preferred spice, however, and the one I suggest you try, is cardamom. Grind the cardamom seeds as finely as you grind the coffee, and put them in with the coffee and sugar right at the beginning. There are usually three seeds in a cardamom pod; start by adding the equivalent of *one seed* (not pod) per demitasse of water, or a "pinch" if the cardamom is pre-ground.

One can hardly call making instant coffee brewing, and I don't have a chapter on mixing and stirring, so I'll have to put my discussion of instant coffees here, as a sort of exemplary afterthought.

INSTANT COFFEE
a word (no more)

I don't wish to insinuate that instant coffee producers are terrible men in tall hats and vests who sneak around in their limousines ripping off the public's birthright—a rich, fragrant cup of real coffee. Instant coffee technologists seem quite passionately involved in their quest for a better instant coffee. And at first glance (not taste) instant coffee does seem to offer many advantages: It stays fresh longer; you can't mess it up as badly as you can regular coffee; it's fast, easy, and clean; it can be mixed by the cup to individual taste; it contains somewhat less caffeine than regularly brewed coffee; and because the instant process neutralizes strong or unusual flavors, the manufacturer can get away with cheaper beans and pass his savings on to the consumer. Without a doubt some instant coffee is the least expensive caffeine high around; it's the coffeeholic's answer to cheap port.

Yet few of these well-publicized advantages prove out. Instant does stay fresher, but grinding your own makes an even fresher cup. Instant is cleaner, but so are TV dinners. And true, it's hard to blow a cup of instant, but if you've read this far you're all experts anyhow. And if it's only speed you're looking for, the one-cup drip I described earlier will give you much better coffee, and just as fast. So for people with ordinary intelligence who have a tongue and a nose, I can't see any reasons except *possibly* cleanliness and a slight edge in price to recommend instant.

dubious advantages

And you don't need it on backpacking or canoeing trips either—open-pot coffee works fine in the wilds and adds no more weight than instant. At five in the morning after brushing the earwigs out of your sleeping bag and

BREWING IT

cleaning up the mess the raccoons made, you *need* a real cup of coffee. About the only advantage to instant is it doesn't attract bears.

Finally, for those who like unusual coffees, dark-roast coffees, in fact, anyone who wants anything except the standard American cup, instant coffee offers *no* viable alternatives. As I pointed out earlier, the "exotic" instant coffee mixes currently in the supermarkets are insipid fabrications; by comparison freeze-dried Colombian is a superior beverage. If you crave variety, you must go back to basics.

insipid fabrications

Once we dismiss the advantages of instant, the advantages of brewed-from-scratch stand out in aromatic taste-tingling relief. Why does instant often taste more like liquid taffy than coffee? The key again is the extremely volatile coffee essence, which provides all the aroma of fresh coffee and most of the flavor. Remember that this oil is developed by roasting, and remains sealed up in little packets in the bean until liberated by grinding and brewing. Once the coffee essence hits the water, it doesn't last long, which is the reason coffee that sits for a while tastes so flat.

Now instant coffee is brewed pretty much the way a gourmet would do it at home: The beans are roasted, immediately ground, and brewed in gigantic percolators, filter urns really. But, when that fresh, hot stuff is dehydrated, what happens? Remember, "dehydrate" means take the water out, and with the water goes—yes, the coffee essence, the minute little droplets of flavor and odor that mean the difference between flavorless, bitter brown water and coffee.

putting the flavor back

But here technology comes clanking over the hill to save the day. If you lose the flavor somewhere along the line, well then we better *put it back in again.* Coffee technologists have long known that a lot of the essential oil literally goes up in smoke out the chimneys of their roasters. So—you guessed it. The instant coffee people condense some of the essential oil lost in roasting, and *put it back in the coffee* just before it's packed. Clever? Also tricky. So much so that even according to industry admissions, the sharp corners of coffee flavor are neutralized—in other words, the instant process makes bad coffee beans taste better, and *good* coffee beans taste bad.

So far I've stuck to concretes like efficiency and price, and fairly clear subjectives, like flavor and aroma. But I feel obligated to add that the ritual of making a true cup of coffee the right way every morning is good for the soul. It cuts down on mindless coffeeholism, and helps to steady the heart for the more complex activities to come. It gets you started with a confident sense that you can at least make a cup of coffee right, and it's always best to start out winning.

"Which brewing method is best?" is a naive question. "Which brewing method is best for me?" is a question to which one can at least approximate an answer. Take just two variables, body and convenience. Coffee made by the Middle Eastern method is heaviest in body, espresso next heaviest, and cold-water coffee lightest in body, with plain filter coffee a close second. Between are ranged the coffees produced by all the other methods: open pot, plunger pot, drip, and so on. Who is to say which is "best"?

WHICH IS BEST?

Even the question of convenience is relative. The cold-water method is clearly most convenient, automatic filter drip close, and Middle Eastern and open pot a remote last. Still, no one can tell my sculptor friend that making coffee without a strainer in a coffee can is bad because it is clumsy and inconvenient; he appreciates the inconvenience; it adds to his satisfaction and takes his mind off the anxieties of his work. One of the principal reasons for drinking coffee in the first place is the esthetic satisfaction of ritual. You ought to not only love the coffee your pot makes, but the pot itself, and all the little things you do with it.

7 ESPRESSO
What it is and how to brew it

ESPRESSO IS several things all at once. It is a unique method of coffee brewing in which hot water is forced under pressure through tightly packed coffee, a cup at a time. It is a roast of coffee, darker brown than the normal American roast, but not quite black. In a larger sense, it is an entire approach to coffee cuisine, involving not only roast and brewing method, but grind and grinder, a technique of heating milk, and a traditional menu of drinks. And in the largest sense of all, it is an atmosphere or mystique: The espresso brewing machine is the spiritual heart and esthetic centerpiece of the European-style café.

an atmosphere or mystique

The espresso system was developed in and for cafés; despite advances in inexpensive home espresso systems one still can not duplicate the finest café espresso or cappuccino in one's kitchen or dining room. You can come close, however, and I discuss the strategy of the attempt in later pages. For now, I want to address myself to the big, shiny café machines.

Fundamentally they make coffee like any other brewer: by steeping ground coffee in hot water. The difference is the *pressure* applied to the hot water. In normal brewing processes the water seeps by gravity down through

ESPRESSO

ground coffee loosely laid over a filter; in the espresso process the water is *forced under pressure* through very finely ground coffee packed tightly over the filter.

advantages of the espresso system
A fast, yet thorough brewing makes the best coffee. If hot water and ground coffee stay in contact too long, the more unpleasant chemicals in the coffee will be extracted, and the pleasant aroma and flavor will evaporate. Hence the superiority of the espresso system: The pressurized water makes almost instant contact with every grain of ground coffee, and just as instantly begins dribbling out into the cup. Another advantage to the café espresso system is freshness. Every cup is instantly brewed in front of you, a moment before you drink it; in most cases the coffee beans are also ground immediately before brewing. Other restaurant brewing methods make anywhere from a pot to an urn at a time from pre-ground coffee, then let it sit, where it loses flavor and aroma to the detriment of the coffee and the advantage of the ambiance.

a simple principle
The oldest café machines and most home espresso machines work on a simple principle. Water is heated to boiling inside a closed tank; a space is left at the top of the tank, where steam gathers. When a valve is opened below the water line, the pressure of the steam trapped at the top of the tank forces hot water out of the valve and down through the coffee. The idea originated with one Louis Bernard Rabaut in 1822, and was first applied to a large café machine by Edward Loysel de Santais in 1843. Santais' machine wowed the Paris Exposition of 1855 by producing "two thousand cups of coffee an hour." More than likely Santais' machine brewed coffee a pot at a time. It remained for some Italians around the turn of the century to modify Santais' invention and turn it into the first modern espresso machine. They decreased the size of the strainer that held the coffee, but increased the number of valves, enabling these "rapid filter" machines to produce several single cups of coffee simultaneously, rather than a single big pot at a time.

Then as now, the espresso operator packed a few teaspoons of very

PREPARING ESPRESSO
1. PACKING THE COFFEE
2. CLAMPING ON THE RECEPTACLE
3. FORCING HOT WATER THROUGH THE COFFEE

finely ground, dark-roast coffee into a little strainer. He clamped the strainer into a receptacle protruding from the side of the machine. When he opened the valve (or in more modern machines when he pulls a handle or pushes a button), hot water was forced through the coffee and into the cup.

The early espresso machines look like shiny steam engines pointed at the ceiling. The round water tank is set on end, and bristles with picturesque spouts, valves, and pressure gauges. These shiny, eagle-topped towers dominated the European café scene until World War II. After the war the new Italian wanted an even stronger cup of coffee to go with his Vespa, and he wanted it faster. The water tank was laid on its side, and concealed inside a streamlined metal cabinet with lines like a Danish-modern jukebox. The simple valve of the old days was replaced with a spring-powered piston that pushed the water through the coffee even harder and faster. The operator, usually a male with shirt rolled up and forearm exposed, depressed a long metal handle. The handle in turn compressed a spring-loaded piston that forced a dose of hot water slowly through the coffee while the handle majestically returned to its original erect position.

the early machines

spring powered

ESPRESSO

hydraulic powered

In the sixties, just when pumping the handles became the signature performance piece for espresso cafés, less dramatic and more automated means for forcing the hot water through the coffee began to appear. The earliest of these no-hands machines were built around simple hydraulic pumps; today's versions heat water separately from the main reservoir, control water temperature and pressure with precision, and flatter the hi-tech pretensions of the eighties with digital read-outs. These push-button machines tend to carry the streamlined look to its extreme. Everything is concealed inside a single, sleek enamel and chrome housing. And all have one feature in common: The operator pushes a button or trips a switch rather than pumping a long handle. The push-button machines are more easily mastered by the novice, since so much of the operation is automated, but do not necessarily make better espresso. Proprietors of some of the best cafés in the San Francisco Bay Area, at any rate, prefer the pump-piston machines because they give the sophisticated operator maximum control over the brewing process.

steaming milk

With the long, gleaming handle perhaps going the way of the running board, one of the best remaining schticks left to the espresso operator is heating and foaming the milk. Espresso is a strong, concentrated coffee, and in accordance with European tradition, many of the drinks in the espresso cuisine combine it with large quantities of milk. If the milk were not heated, it would instantly cool the coffee. Early in the history of the espresso machine someone realized that the steam collected in the top of the tank could be used to heat milk as well as provide pressure for coffee making. A valve with a long nozzle was let into the upper part of the tank where the steam gathers. When the valve is opened by unscrewing a knob, the compressed steam comes hissing out of the end of the nozzle. Cold milk is poured into a pitcher; the espresso operator shoves the nozzle into the milk and opens the valve. The compressed steam shoots out through the milk, both heating it and raising an attractive head of froth or foam.

Café patrons soon discovered that steamed, frothed milk both tastes

ESPRESSO

and looks better than milk heated in the ordinary way, and it became an important part of espresso cuisine. The white head of foam is decorative, can be garnished with a dash of cocoa or cinnamon, prevents a skin from forming on the surface of the milk, and insulates the hot coffee.

European tastes

It is difficult to say how much of the success of the espresso machine is owing to its scientifically impeccable approach to coffee making, or its drama and novelty, but given European tastes it certainly does put out a remarkable cup of coffee: absolutely freshly ground and freshly brewed, and so quickly brewed that, as an Italian friend of mine says, you get only the *heart* of the coffee.

Nevertheless, many a mainstream American coffee lover facing a cup of espresso for the first time may take one swallow, and either finish it stoically or hide the little cup behind his napkin. His distaste is understandable: This impeccable brewing system is designed to make a cup of coffee in the southern European or Latin American tradition, rather than the northern European or North American. Good espresso is rich, heavy-bodied, almost syrupy, and has the characteristic bittersweet bite of dark-roasted coffee. Its sharp flavor and heavy body make it an ideal coffee to be drunk with milk and sugar, but hardly the sort of beverage to be drunk unsweetened, or in large quantities.

cappuccino

Most espresso drinkers outside Italy prefer a cappuccino, a drink made of about one-third espresso and two-thirds hot milk and foam. The milk dilutes and mellows the strong, sharp coffee. With a home espresso machine, one can use a lighter-roasted coffee and come out with a drink with the same richness as café espresso, but without the dark-roasted tang.

Southern Europeans have drunk strong, sharply flavored coffee in small cups or mixed with hot milk for generations. Consequently, most of the drinks in the espresso cuisine are not original with the machine; rather, the machine brought them from promise to perfection. Here are some of the most popular:

Espresso A single demitasse (about one and one-half ounces) of espresso coffee, black, usually drunk with sugar. Can be flavored with a drop or two of almond or tangerine extract.

Espresso Romano A demitasse of espresso served with a twist or a thin slice of lemon on the side.

Espresso Ristretto "Restricted" or short espresso. Carries the "small is beautiful" espresso philosophy to its ultimate: The flow of espresso is cut short at about one ounce, producing an even denser and more perfumy cup of espresso than the norm.

Double or Doppio A full six-ounce cup of straight espresso. To be drunk only by veteran espresso bibbers, early in the morning, before a 12-hour work day and a long evening.

Cappuccino (French: *café crème*) About one-third espresso, one-third hot milk, topped with one-third foam, in a heavy cup. Like the others, usually drunk with sugar.

Caffè Latte (French: *café au lait;* Spanish: *café con leche*) One or two shots of espresso, and three times as much frothed milk, in a big bowl or wide-mouthed glass. This is the favored breakfast drink of southern Europeans, and is never drunk past noon by anyone except children and Americans. Caffè Latte has a greater proportion of milk to coffee than a cappuccino, and tastes weaker and milkier. Strictly speaking, the milk and coffee should be poured simultaneously, one from either side of the bowl. The hot milk and coffee are often served separately in Europe.

Espresso Macchiato A demitasse of espresso "marked" (*macchiato*) with a small quantity of hot, frothed milk.

Latte Macchiato A glass half-filled with hot, frothed milk, into which a demitasse of espresso is slowly dribbled. The coffee will color the milk in faint, graduated layers, darker at the top shading to light at the bottom, all contrasting to the layer of pure white foam at the top.

Mocha Not to be confused with Mocha-Java, a traditional American-roasted blend of Mocha and Java coffees. A mocha to an espresso aficionado is about one-third espresso, one-third strong, unsweetened hot chocolate, and

ESPRESSO

one-third steamed milk. The milk goes in last, and the whole thing is usually served in a mug. Voltaire is said to have consumed 40 cups of mocha a day at the Café Procope.

garnishing the foam

Some cafés garnish the froth of the cappuccino and caffè latte with a dash of unsweetened cocoa, which adds the subtle perfume of chocolate to the drink. Others use cinnamon, which I don't approve of; I find it too distinctive a flavor and out of harmony with the dark tones of the coffee. Straight espresso is delicious with whipped cream *(con panna),* but topping a good, foamy cappuccino with whipped cream is as pointless as putting catsup on spaghetti.

alleged cappuccino

Unfortunately, few North American coffee drinkers have an opportunity to experience the extraordinary perfume of the true espresso coffee. Many of the alleged cappuccini I've tasted outside the best cafés of San Francisco or New York resemble a somewhat superior version of instant coffee and hot milk, and even the best still ruin the espresso component by overextraction. Sometimes café owners load a lot of canned whipped cream and cinnamon on top in an apparent effort to romanticize the grim reality underneath. The art of cappuccino, as practiced in the espresso bars of Italy, is a gesture of pure truth, transcendent. Tasting one makes me want to start praising God, or at least applauding vigorously.

principal mistakes

The two principal mistakes I've observed being committed by espresso operators are using a preground coffee and letting too much water run through the grounds. The purpose of the espresso system is to produce an absolutely fresh cup of coffee, custom brewed on demand. Using a preground, canned coffee, rather than fresh-ground coffee from the matched grinders made to accompany the big machines, defeats this system at its source. And allowing too much water to flow through even fresh-ground coffee will produce a thin, bitter cup. The espresso system is so efficient that the goodness is extracted from the ground coffee almost immediately, producing, as I've said, a small amount of intense brew, usually no more than an ounce-and-a-half per serving. If you want more quantity in your

STEAM

WATER

cup, then you should drink another style of coffee or order a cappuccino, which mixes the small amount of intense coffee with two or three times as much milk.

ESPRESSO
AT HOME

If you *have* tasted a really fine espresso or cappuccino, however, and you want more, you may want to cut out the restaurateurs and make your own. In this case, your first step should be deciding what you like about it. For instance, if you like the pungent *flavor* of the espresso and are indifferent to the rich texture of the coffee itself, or the effect of frothed milk, then you may be just as happy with dark-roasted coffee, made in the ordinary way. Start with a half a pound of the darkest roast in the store, ground for your regular coffee maker.

If you simply want a strong European-style coffee for brandy and whiskey drinks, you can purchase one of the many inexpensive espresso brewers *without* steam valves, described below. Make sure you read my instructions on making espresso, however, since used unknowledgeably these objects can make very bad coffee.

But if you like the rich, creamy texture of straight espresso, or if you like steamed milk with your espresso, then study the chart that appears later in this chapter describing the options for a home espresso machine. But before you review the range of machines available and their capabilities, you may need a review of espresso fundamentals.

espresso roast

First the coffee. The standard espresso roast, also called Italian and sometimes French, is a good place to start. But remember that you can make any coffee in your espresso maker, so long as the beans are properly ground. You may want a coffee darker than espresso roast, or lighter. No matter what coffee you choose, you will always come out with the rich texture and heavy body of espresso. But only with the darker roasts will you come out with the sweet, rich tang of true café espresso. In general, use as much coffee as is needed to fill the coffee receptacle of your machine. If in doubt, use two level tablespoons of finely ground coffee for every demitasse of espresso.

There are two requirements to making good home espresso. First, you need to grind your coffee just fine enough, and tamp it down in the receptacle just hard enough, so the water is forced through the coffee *slowly*. Second, you need to stop the brewing process at just the correct moment. The more expensive the machine, the more sophisticated will be the method for controlling the flow of hot water through the coffee. To return to the first point: If the coffee is ground finely enough and tamped properly, you'll come out with a dark, rich, sweet brew, topped with the delicate brown froth that marks your espresso as the real stuff. If the coffee is ground too coarsely or not packed down hard enough, the water will come gushing through, and you'll end up with watery, bitter stuff that will send you and your guests back to the percolator. If the coffee is ground *too* finely or packed *too* tightly, nothing at all may happen. Or if you are using a stove-top machine, the trapped steam could pop the safety valve and fill your kitchen with an explosive hiss, indicating you have quite literally blown it by not allowing *any* water to penetrate the coffee.

the right grind

The best grind is very fine, gritty, but *not* a dusty powder. If you look at the ground coffee from a foot away, you barely should be able to distinguish particles. If you rub some between your fingers, it should feel gritty. Most canned espresso coffees, like Medaglia D'Oro or Motta, are ground much too coarsely. Your best bet as usual is your own grinder. If you have whole beans ground at the store, ask for a very fine grind, for an espresso machine.

Fill the receptacle with coffee to the indicated point (or to the brim if there is no indication), then *lightly* and *evenly* tamp it down. Don't hammer on it, just lightly tamp. If you fear the grind is too coarse, tamp a little more heavily; if too fine, tamp lightly or not at all. Never use less than the minimum volume of ground coffee indicated for your machine, even if you are brewing a single cup. If the coffee gushes out, rather than dribbles out,

tamping it

compensate by using a finer grind of coffee, or by tamping the coffee down more firmly.

The richest espresso comes out right at the beginning; as brewing continues it becomes progressively thinner and more bitter. Collect only as much coffee as you will actually serve. If your brewer has no mechanism for cutting off the flow of the coffee, improvise: Remove the machine from the heat when enough coffee has flowed out, or replace the coffee-collecting receptacle with a second receptacle to catch the excess coffee. Whatever you do, don't spoil the first bloom of coffee with the pale and bitter dregs.

FROTHING MILK

Most Americans prefer their espresso blended with hot, frothed milk as cappuccino or caffè latte. Fortunately, most espresso-brewing appliances sold in the United States now have built-in steam valves, suitable for the milk-frothing operation.

There are three steps to making an espresso drink with frothed milk. The first is making the coffee; the second is frothing and heating the milk; the third is combining the two. Never froth the coffee and the milk together; such slipshod democracy would stale the fresh coffee and ruin the eye-pleasing contrast between the white foam and dark coffee.

in a cup or pitcher

So assume the coffee is made. You can either froth the milk in the cups before you add the coffee, or in a separate pitcher. Either way, fill the cup or container about halfway with cold milk (the colder the better; hot milk will not produce foam). The steam jet is a little pipe which protrudes from the top or side of your machine, with a screw knob for opening or closing it. When one is making coffee, one normally keeps this valve screwed closed. On the tip of the steam jet are two to four little holes, which project steam downward and diagonally, in little jets. Open the steam valve just a crack before you insert the nozzle into the pitcher, to prevent milk from being sucked back up into the tube.

Heating the milk is easy; getting a head of foam is a little trickier, and like centering the clay on a potter's wheel, difficult to explain in words.

STEAMING MILK
1. INSERTING THE STEAM JET AND OPENING THE VALVE
2. FROTHING THE MILK 3. HEATING THE MILK

First thrust the nozzle deeply into the milk. Then open the valve a couple of turns, and close it again gradually until you get a strong, but not explosive, hiss of steam. Now lower the milk container until the steam starts bubbling or hissing *just below the surface of the milk*. If you have the nozzle too deeply into the milk there will be no hiss or bubble; if you have it too shallow it will spray milk all over the kitchen. If you have it just right, a gratifying head of foam will begin rising from the surface of the milk. You will need to follow the foam upward as it develops; listen for the hiss; if it turns to dull rumble you are too deep in the milk.

After you have a good head of foam, feel the sides of the container to see if the milk is hot enough. If not, lower the nozzle to the bottom of the container and keep it there until the sides heat up. Never boil the milk, and *always froth the milk first*, before you heat it, since cold milk froths best.

heating milk

If you get a few big bubbles, rather than the many tiny ones which go to make up a strong, stable head of foam, either knock the bottom of the pitcher on the counter or let it sit for a minute before you combine the milk with the coffee. If you are using a stove-top machine and the jet of steam is too weak to really churn the milk around, raise the heat slightly and make certain no pressure is escaping through the coffee valve.

ESPRESSO

CHOOSING
A HOME ESPRESSO
MACHINE

If you are still tempted by the idea of a home espresso machine after all of my fussy directions and detailed admonitions, begin by studying the charts on the following pages.

Recall that the creamy heaviness and rich flavor of espresso are owing to a rapid and thorough extraction of the flavor oils from the coffee, achieved by forcing hot water *under pressure* through the resistance of fresh, finely ground, compacted coffee. The espresso brewers in the first four categories of my chart generate the requisite water pressure through the simple means described earlier: the natural pressure of trapped steam. Look at the cutaway illustration of a simple espresso pot on page 139. There is a water reservoir above a heat source, a receptacle to receive the brewed coffee above or to the side of the reservoir, and between the two a container for the ground coffee. Steam trapped in the water reservoir presses down on the boiling water, forcing it up through the barrier of finely ground coffee, and it dribbles out espresso.

Brewers in Category 1 are so limited in nature that they barely qualify as espresso makers. Since they offer no means of cutting off the flow of

stove-top machines

coffee, one must hover over the machine and manage to remove it from the heat at precisely the right moment to prevent an excessive flow of water through the coffee and a thin, bitter, overextracted brew. More importantly for the average cappuccino-leaning American espresso drinker, these machines have no valve stem for frothing and heating milk. The only reason I can think of for buying one is to stare at it after dinner. The Alessi is rightly enshrined in the collection of New York's Museum of Modern Art, the Vesuviana implies arias, and the Contessa looks like something lifted from a Florentine palazzo.

Machines in Category 2 are another matter. They are not easy to use either, but with study and attention will produce good Italian coffee drinks, both with and without frothed milk. They work on the same simple steam-pressure principle as those in Category 1, but have a valve which taps the steam in the reservoir for frothing milk, and a second valve for cutting off

STOVE-TOP ESPRESSO MACHINES
Brewing pressure provided by natural buildup of steam pressure in water reservoir

I WITHOUT VALVE FOR FROTHING AND HEATING MILK; WITHOUT MECHANISM FOR CONTROLLING COFFEE OUTPUT

BREWED COFFEE

GROUND COFFEE

WATER RESERVOIR

Moka Espress ($16/$12)
Siesta, etc. ($30/$24)
Alessi ($55/$50)
Kontessa ($75)

Advantages: Some models are very inexpensive; others are very attractive.

Disadvantages: Cannot be used to make coffee drinks using frothed milk; almost impossible to achieve quality espresso; can only brew multiple cups.

2 WITH VALVE FOR FROTHING AND HEATING MILK; WITH MECHANISM FOR CONTROLLING COFFEE OUTPUT

Italian Espress ($30/$22)
National Houseware ($35/$28)
Via Veneto ($63/$50)
Atomic ($90/$85)
Signor Cappuccino II, with
   tabletop heating element ($115/$70)

Advantages: Inexpensive; easy to store; can be used to froth milk or prepare hot chocolate independent of the coffee-making operation.

Disadvantages: Difficult to achieve quality espresso; can only brew multiple cups.

the flow of coffee. These permit the vigilant operator to manage the coffee production with precision and claim the heart of the coffee for his drink, without diluting it with the pale dregs.

trick to these machines

As I indicated earlier, the trick to machines in the first two categories is to use the perfect grind of coffee: one capable of resisting the flow of hot water sufficiently to build up a sturdy degree of steam pressure, but not so powdery as to stop the flow of water altogether. This balance can only be obtained through trial and error. If the coffee is ground to a grit (not a powder) and properly tamped, the coffee will dribble richly at first, then dribble palely, then gush. All you need do is cut the coffee flow off near the end of the richly dribbling phase to capture the essence of the coffee without watery and bitter afterthoughts. If your coffee gushes right from the beginning, first make certain you are *filling* the coffee receptacle as indicated by the manufacturer, and lightly tamping the coffee down. If it still gushes, use a finer grind, *but never an absolute powder.*

operating sequence

Again, the correct operating sequence for most machines is to keep the steam valve closed while you are making coffee, then begin the milk frothing and heating operation after you have finished your brewing. A few machines may call for both operations to take place at the same time. Obviously, *never close both valves when the machine is on the heat.* All of these stove-top machines have efficient pressure escape valves. But there is always the danger of valve malfunction and a sudden release of steam pressure if you leave a machine on the heat with all valves closed. If you need to interrupt the frothing procedure to answer the phone, leave the milk-frothing valve cracked open. Not only will pressure be relieved while you are gone, but the hissing will remind you that you have unfinished business in the kitchen.

All of the machines listed in Category 2 are fairly similar in design and material except the Atomic, a lovable, eccentric piece of machinery, which looks like a cross between an overstuffed chair and a 1950 Ford. I own an Atomic and love it, but can't wholeheartedly recommend it because

COUNTERTOP ELECTRIC ESPRESSO MACHINES
Brewing pressure provided by natural buildup of steam pressure in water reservoir

3 WITH VALVE FOR FROTHING AND HEATING MILK; WITHOUT MECHANISM FOR CONTROLLING COFFEE OUTPUT

Krups Mini ($90/$60)
Maxim ($80/$40)

Advantages: Inexpensive; easier to achieve quality espresso than with stovetop models.

Disadvantages: Nevertheless require close attention to make good espresso; occupy some counter space; Maxim cannot be used to froth milk or prepare hot chocolate independent of the coffee-making operation.

4 WITH VALVE FOR FROTHING AND HEATING MILK; WITH MECHANISM FOR CONTROLLING COFFEE OUTPUT

Piccola ($70/$50)

Advantages: Same as 3, but brewing operation can be controlled with greater precision; *can* be used to froth milk or prepare hot chocolate independent of the coffee-making operation.

Disadvantages: Requires close attention to make good espresso; occupies some counter space.

ESPRESSO

of its material (aluminum) and the ineffective means for controlling the coffee flow (a brass pin inserted across the coffee outlet opening).

Machines in Category 3 and Category 4 are probably the best bet for the espresso lover on a budget. Like the machines in the first two categories, they use the accumulated pressure of trapped steam to force the water through the coffee. But unlike the stove-top styles they contain a built-in electric element that ensures a safer machine with a more consistent operation. Furthermore, the receptacle for the ground coffee is contained in a detachable holder, as it is in the large café machines, making the machine easier to load and keep clean.

counter-top electric machines

The Piccola, Category 4, has a valve for controlling the flow of hot water through the coffee, much like the machines in Category 2. On the other hand, the Category 3 machines (Krups and Maxim) do not have such a valve. Thus we are back to a situation wherein the operator needs to improvise a method for picking off the best of the espresso. The manufacturer of the Krups machine suggests loading just enough water to achieve the amount of espresso you want. That's a start, but I also suggest replacing the coffee receptacle with a second receptacle (a small ceramic cup, for example), when just enough espresso has been produced to satisfy your needs. The excess will run into the second cup while you're steaming milk.

I recommend the Krups (despite its inconvenient lack of a coffee control valve) over both the Piccola and the Maxim. The Krups machine appears to be better made and puts out a stronger flow of steam for frothing milk. Frothing milk on these small electric machines, by the way, requires more skill than needed with the stove-top machines, since the steam pressure may not be as explosive as can be obtained by raising the heat under one of the stove-top styles. The gain in consistency and safety, however, is probably worth the extra effort in developing a good frothing technique.

With the fifth and sixth categories we enter the world of the true espresso machine. These miniature versions of the café giants produce more consistent coffee than the smaller machines, and require less fuss and atten-

5 HAND-OPERATED PISTON ESPRESSO MACHINES
Countertop electric; hand-operated piston intensifies brewing pressure

WITH VALVE FOR FROTHING AND HEATING MILK; HAND-OPERATED PISTON CONTROLS COFFEE OUTPUT

> La Pavoni Europiccola ($400/$300)
> Olympia Cremina ($400/$300)
> Riviera ($500/$450)

Advantages: Even a beginner can produce quality espresso; robust steam pressure; varying pressure on piston handle can compensate for varying grinds of coffee; can produce single cups; pumping the piston is provocative and conversation inducing.

Disadvantages: Expensive; slow to heat up; must be cooled to refill; reservoir must be emptied if machine is not used regularly; occupies counter space.

6 SWITCH-ACTIVATED PUMP ESPRESSO MACHINES

Countertop electric.

WITH VALVE FOR FROTHING AND HEATING MILK; SWITCH- OR BUTTON-ACTIVATED PUMP SYSTEM CONTROLS COFFEE OUTPUT

Avanti Minibar ($130/$100)	Coffee Gaggia ($200/$180)
Elespresso ($160/$130)	Krups Espresso Novo ($275/$190)
Faema Ciao ($200/$180)	Olympia Coffex ($500/$400)

Advantages: Even a beginner can produce quality espresso; can produce single cups; most models can be refilled while in use and reservoirs do not need to be emptied between sessions.

Disadvantages: Expensive; automation makes the brewing process less dramatic and possibly less subject to operator control than the pump piston; occupies counter space.

tion along the way. The chart indicates the difference between the two categories: The machines in Category 5 have a manual piston, while those in Category 6 use a switch-activated pump to control coffee flow and generate brewing pressure. The Category 5 machines look like the old-time pump café machines, but work differently. There is no spring-loaded piston, as in the café machines; instead there is a direct relationship between handle and piston—as you pull down on the handle the piston forces hot water through the coffee. Machines in this category are sturdy, well made, and redolent with old-time café nostalgia. But since they heat up an entire reservoir (four to 24 cups) of water at a time, they are slow to achieve brewing temperature (10 to 15 minutes). And because the entire tank of water is heated, they must be cooled to be refilled.

manual piston machines

Category 6 machines are automated, replacing the pull-down handle with a switch-activated pump. Furthermore, most of the Category 6 machines heat water in small batches separate from the main reservoir. This means fast start-up and a reservoir that can be refilled while the machine is in use, without cooling or interrupting the brewing cycle.

switch-activated pumps

Even with these sophisticated machines you must make sure to obtain the correct gritty grind of coffee, fill the receptacle to the point indicated, and spread and tamp the coffee. Since these machines are rather large, complex appliances, they do not automatically transfer heat to the components that hold the coffee: the coffee receptacle, the holder, and the gruppo (the fixture into which the holder clamps). Consequently, these components should be preheated by running a dose of hot water through them at the start of a brewing session.

As for recommendations, I like the Elespress for price and quality. For people who entertain, for offices, or for extended families of espresso drinkers, I recommend either the Olympia Cremina or the Olympia Coffex for their solid durability and large capacity. For the old-fashioned romantic, I recommend the Pavoni Europiccola, which bristles with shiny tubes and dials. (Available directly from Thomas Cara in San Francisco; see Resources.) The Coffee Gaggia and the Krups Espresso Novo also look like good machines, although I have not had direct experience with them. The Avanti Minibar appears flimsy; if you're shopping for price, I'd recommend spending a little more for the Elespress. If you can't locate the Elespress in your area, you can arrange to purchase one by mail through Peet's Coffee in Berkeley, California (see Resources).

As you may have gathered by my obsessive yammering about the importance of the correct grind of coffee in brewing espresso, the grinder is as important a piece of equipment as the espresso brewer itself. With grinders, as with the brewing machines, the more you pay the less you need to know. A simple blade grinder like the $24 Bosch recommended on page 91 will produce an excellent espresso grind, if you use it properly: that is, if you don't load it up with too many beans; if you grind in short spurts, bouncing the grinder between spurts to knock the larger pieces of coffee back down around the blades; and if you stop at the right moment, when you have a grit just short of powder. On the other extreme, the $100-and-up specialized espresso grinders will maintain the setting for the correct grind session after session, will measure one-cup doses of coffee at the flick of a lever, and may even have a projecting component designed to make tamping the coffee a casual, one-handed operation. Between these extremes are the less-expensive, general-purpose, burr-style mills, like the Braun described on page 88. Such machines maintain a fairly consistent grind, but need to be cleaned regularly and generally babied.

ESPRESSO GRINDERS

Many manufacturers make entire miniature coffee bars, with matching espresso machine, grinder, and a tray with a café-style drawer into which one knocks the spent coffee grounds. The three-piece Coffee Gaggia set, for example, sells for around $300. For those with money to spend and a taste for consistent espresso, these little outfits are worth the money, particularly for those who want to break a terminal café habit.

miniature coffee bars

ARAB COFFEE SHOP

8 SERVING IT

The social sacrament; from Arabian coffee ceremony to thermos jug

RITUAL OFTEN CHOOSES for its vehicle consciousness-altering substances like alcohol, marijuana, or coffee. Primitive cultures often assume a bit of God resides in these substances, because through them we are separated for a moment from the ordinariness of things, and somehow seize our own reality more clearly. This is why so many rituals are, besides a gesture of hospitality and reassurance, a celebration of a break in routine, a moment when the human drive for survival lets up, and we simply *are*, together. This last is to me the real meaning of the coffee break, the coffee klatsch, the happy hour, the beer bust, and the after-dinner coffee. These are secular rituals that in unobtrusive, essential ways help maintain our humanness with one another and with ourselves.

In many cultures the ritual aspects of drinking tea or coffee, or smoking tobacco, are given a semireligious status. The most famous of such rituals is the Japanese tea ceremony, in which a strong powdered green tea is whipped in an ancient bowl to form a rich frothy drink, which is then ceremonially passed, in total silence, from one participant to the next. The tea ceremony is quite consciously structured as a sort of communal meditation,

rituals

147

SERVING IT

a few minutes devoted to contemplating the presence of eternity in the moment. Doubtless the caffeine in the tea aids in such psychic enterprise.

Allowed to degenerate, however, such rituals simply become excuses to display our ancient tea bowls, deco martini pitchers, or new $500 espresso machines. It is the whiff of the eternal in the present, shared with ourselves or others, that ultimately justifies all this artistic gear.

witchcraft and fertility

Coffee from the beginning has been one of humanity's sacramental substances. In Africa, for instance, it is used in witchcraft and fertility rites. Fredrick Wellman, in *Coffee: Botany, Cultivation, and Utilization,* describes an African blood brother ceremony in which "blood of the two pledging parties is mixed and put between the twin seeds of a coffee fruit and the whole swallowed."

Coffee in its hot, black, modern form was first used as a medicine, next as an aid to prayer and meditation by Arabian monastics, much as green tea is used by Zen monks in Japan to celebrate and fortify. Pilgrims to Mecca then carried coffee all over the Moslem world, and it became secularized, but the religious association remained. Some Christians were at first wont to brand coffee as "that blacke bitter invention of Satan," as opposed to good Christian wine, but the 16th century Pope Clement VIII is said to have sampled the stuff, and declaring it was too good to let the Moslems have it all, gave it his official blessing.

With the Moslems, however, particularly with the Arabs, coffee has maintained its religious connotation, and the ritual aspects apparently remain refined and conscious. There is, in fact, an Arabian coffee ceremony, which, had American intellectuals turned to Arabia rather than to Japan for a modern philosophy of art, might rival the tea ceremony in influence. It is very similar, and properly performed, doubtlessly as beautiful.

coffee ceremony

But on a less-conscious level, a hundred thousand coffee ceremonies take place simultaneously all over the world: in office lunch rooms, in espresso bars, in Swedish parlors, in Japanese coffee houses, wherever coffee drinkers gather to stare into space, to read a newspaper, or to share a moment, outside time and obligation, with their friends.

Ritual is further wrapped up in the smell and taste of coffee itself. Certain smells, flavors, movements, sounds combine to symbolize *coffee* and suggest a mood of contemplation or well-being in an entire culture. This, I'm convinced, was the reason for the persistence of the pumping percolator in American culture: To an American in 1950, it *sounded* and *smelled* like coffee, and made us feel good before we even lifted a cup.

Other cultures have similarly arbitrary associations: To a Middle Easterner, the foam that gathers in the pot when he cooks his coffee is an indispensable part of the drink, not because it tastes good, but because it symbolizes the meditative glow of *coffee*. Italian and other hard-core espresso aficionados put a similar, if somewhat less ceremonial, emphasis on foam. An Italian will not take a cup of espresso seriously if it isn't topped with a thin layer of what to a filter-coffee drinker probably looks like brown scum; the foam is what marks it as the real thing. A similar satisfaction resides in the foamy milk that tops drinks like caffè latte or cappuccino. True, the foam has no flavor, but a cappuccino is not a cappuccino without it.

foam

Ritual is what gives validity to the extraordinary variety of cups, pots, and paraphernalia human beings have developed simply to transport coffee from the pot to the palate. There are of course practical matters involved,

SERVING IT

notably keeping the coffee hot on the way, but most variations are refinements that solely answer the very real need for the satisfaction of ritual. Of course, there is nothing to stop people from buying new gadgets or fancy pots in order to produce a Christmas present or a big impression, but purchases made for the wrong reason usually carry their own roundabout retribution. Call it garage sale karma. If you don't really care about espresso, for example, your new machine doubtless will end up in the driveway some Sunday selling for $5.

Again, the only practical contribution serving paraphernalia can make to our coffee-drinking pleasure is keeping the coffee hot. Obviously you *keeping it hot* can do this two ways: provide a heat source, or keep the coffee in a container which retains heat. A continuing heat source is virtually indispensible with Melitta, Chemex, and other filter brewers, since the brewing process takes so long. Most filter brewers can't be put directly on the burner, and you would risk boiling or overheating your coffee anyhow; you need to buffer the heat with either a heat-reducing pad or a hot-water bath. If you are not concerned with esthetics you can simply immerse the bottom part of your filter coffee maker in a pot of hot water. Chemex offers a heat-reducing grid, and you can usually find a Mouli Radiant Heat Plate in any cooking-gear shop for about $4.

If you want to keep your filter coffee warm at the table, you can choose between an adjustable electic warmer, a candle warmer, or a warmer especially made for coffee makers, like the Melitta ($13) or Chemex ($25).

Covered pots for serving coffee have been in vogue since the Arabs started drinking it. At import stores you can still find the traditional Arabian serving pot, with it "S"-shaped spout, Aladdin's lamp pedestal and *covered pots* pointed cover. You can also occasionally find an *ibrik*, or Middle Eastern coffee maker, with an embossed cover for keeping the coffee hot between servings. The changes in English coffee-pot design are fascinating. On one hand stands the severe, straight-sided pewter pot of the 17th century, which suggests a Puritan in his stiff collar; on the other, the silver coffee pots of the Romantic revival, which take the original Arabian design and make it seethe with enough squiggles and flourishes to fulfill the most ardent fantasies of a romantic nobleman should he glance up from the latest gothic fiction to contemplate the imitation oriental splendor of his sitting room reflected in the shimmering arabesques of his coffee pot.

Ever since, coffee-server design has wobbled between these two extremes. In the past two decades the coffee pot and matching sugar dish and creamer have been out of fashion, but are making a modest comeback, right next to the martini pitcher and the cocktail shaker. Always favored by the esoteric few, the Continental-style coffee server is an excellent choice for the coffee ritualist. It is smaller than the English-style pot, and has a straight handle protruding from the body of the pot like an arrow sticking out of a cowboy. The French often serve the coffee part of café au lait in a pot of this kind, and put the hot milk in another small, open-topped pitcher. One picks up the coffee in one hand and the milk in another, and pours both into the bowl simultaneously, in one smooth gesture. The straight handle, which points toward you and rolls in your hand as you

continental-style server

151

pour, makes this important operation easier to manage. I've seen these pots in copper for around $20.

The space-age contribution to coffee serving is the thermos; it works like the old thermos jug, but has a bit more class. The serving thermos keeps coffee hot for hours, and though the aroma goes quickly, the flavor holds well. A family which eats breakfast in shifts, or anyone who likes to keep his coffee hot for an hour or two or more, might want to purchase a serving thermos. It is much easier on flavor than reheating. The cheapest ($15 to $20) are all plastic and have a bright, aggressive contemporary chic. Stainless-steel models, also with a contemporary look, sell for $20 to $25, and traditional-look brass or silver plate for $60 and up. The top of the line is probably the Zitzmann silver thermal carafe, which retails through Hammacher Schlemmer in New York for $100 in the half-liter size and $130 for the liter.

Coffee is probably best served in heavy ceramic mugs or cups that have been warmed first with a little hot water. There are many directions to take: fancy china, deco and moderne revivals, new-wave whimsy, folksy hand-thrown earthenware, cheaper machine-made mugs which look hand-thrown, heavy classic mugs and cups from restaurant suppliers, and lately, imported restaurant ware from Europe. I prefer the restaurant-supply ware; it looks solid, feels authentic, reflects the hearty democratic tradition of coffee, and bounces when you drop it.

demitasse Straight espresso, after-dinner coffees brewed double-strength, and Middle Eastern coffees are traditionally served in a half-size, or demitasse cup. There seems to be something perfectly appropriate to drinking such intense, perfumy stuff out of small cups rather than from the usual ingratiatingly generous mugs and cups. You should have the small demitasse spoons to go with the cups; an ordinary spoon looks like a shovel next to a demitasse cup. You can save considerable money on such gear at a restaurant-supply store. A set of stainless-steel demitasse spoons, for instance, will cost one-tenth what they will anywhere else, and if they don't look good enough to you,

you probably have enough money to buy sterling. Nearly every espresso specialty—cappuccino, mocha, caffè latte—has its preferred style of cup, mug, or glass; I introduce them along with the drinks in Chapter 7.

German and Scandinavian tradition calls for paper-thin porcelain cups, to go with the water-thin coffee served at the traditional *Kaffeeklatsch.* Andres Uribe, in his book *Brown Gold,* claims the ladies at the original German *Kaffeeklatschen* called their coffee *Blumechenkaffee,* "flower-coffee," after the little painted flowers which their thin, tea-like beverage permitted them to see all too clearly at the bottom of their Dresden cups.

When I was a teenager in the Midwest circa 1955, drinking your coffee any other way than black made your manhood suspect, or your dates wonder whether you were the kind of woman who ate two-pound boxes of chocolate while reading movie magazines. People would leer patronizingly at you, and tell you that you couldn't possibly like coffee that much if you had to add cream and sugar to it. I assume they didn't like beef, since most of them ate it cooked and seasoned. Perhaps the forties and fifties preference for thin, black coffee went along with an equivalent love of characterless white wines, dry martinis, and lager beer. It's as though to admit to liking sweet, heavy drinks was tantamount to admitting some unpardonable weakness, like a penchant for Perry Como or cocker spaniels.

MILK AND SUGAR
the great debate

unpardonable weakness

One reason for the prejudice in the United States against milk in coffee may be the prevailing style of the coffee: If you add *anything* to the average cup of thin, under-flavored stuff they serve in many restaurants, you eliminate what little there was to taste in the first place. On the other hand, dark-roasted European-style coffees, and all the great rich, full-bodied coffees of the world, brewed correctly, will carry their flavor intact through nearly any amount of milk. Too much milk, of course, will cool the coffee, unless you heat it, or better yet, steam it the way European-style cafés do. Anyone who enjoys milk in his coffee might consider purchasing a milk steamer like the one described in Chapter 7.

9 CAFFEINE
The caffeine controversy
and decaffeinated coffees

WHEN SIR WILLIAM HARVEY, the 17th-century physician credited with discovering the circulation of the blood, was on his death bed, he allegedly called his lawyer to his side and held up a coffee bean. "This little Fruit," he whispered, eyes doubtless still bright from his morning cup, "is the source of happiness and wit!" Sir William then bequeathed his entire supply of coffee, 56 pounds, to the London College of Physicians, directing them to commemorate the day of his death every month with a morning round of coffee.

To some of a puritan or suspicious nature, this anecdote may strike a sinister note. Did Sir William die young? How *much* coffee did he drink, and did he have any enemies in the College of Physicians?

a sinister note

Paradox runs through the entire history of coffee. It began as medicine, and graduated to simultaneous roles as panacea and poison. Early in its history, for instance, coffee was adopted by Arabian dervishes to fortify their religious meditation. Yet no more than 50 years later, in Mecca, it was the subject of vehement religious persecutions on grounds it encouraged mirth and chess-playing among the faithful. Religion still can't make up its mind about coffee; Mormons and some fundamentalists reject it, while most

CAFFEINE

Moslems and many Christians consider it a sober and wholesome alternative to wine and spirits.

In the 17th century, when religion gave way to science and priests to doctors, the debate continued. One physician claimed coffee relieved dropsy, gravel, gout, migraine, hypochondria, and cured scurvy outright, while another declared that drunk with milk, it caused leprosy. "The lovers of coffee used the physicians very ill when they met together," says one detached French observer, "and the physicians on their side threatened the coffee drinkers with all sorts of diseases."

an unsettling accusation

One of the most unsettling accusations leveled against coffee came in a tale by a 17th-century German traveler, Adam Oelshlager, in his *Relation of a Voyage to Muscovie, Tartary, and Persia.* The story concerns the king of Persia, who "had become so habituated to the use of coffee that he took a dislike for women." One day the queen saw a stallion being emasculated; upon asking the reason she was told the animal was too spirited, and was being gelded to tame it. Whereupon the queen suggested a simpler solution would be to feed it coffee every morning. This story, when introduced into southern France, was said to have virtually ruined the coffee trade there for 50 years. On the other hand, a tale from a Persian saga reports that after the prophet Mohammed had his first cup of coffee (delivered by the angel Gabriel), he "felt able to unseat forty horsemen and possess fifty women."

aphrodisiac

I leave the relationship between coffee and potency to my readers and Dr. Ruth, but I can't help but note that one of capitalism's minor ventures into sexual enlightenment, an over-the-counter aphrodisiac or "sexual stimulation tablet," contained 100 milligrams of caffeine, along with ginseng powder and vitamin E. The latter two ingredients, however healthful, have doubtless considerably less effect than the caffeine on the matter immediately in hand.

It was in England of the 17th century that coffee's career as medicine reached its apex, and possibly, nadir. The most extravagant claims were launched for its medicinal value, and the most extraordinary accusations leveled against it. One Englishman named Walter Rumsey invented an "electuary" of coffee, to be taken internally with the aid of an instrument called a "provang." The "electuary" was prescribed for intestinal disorders and hysteria. First one prepared the electuary, which consisted of heated butter, salad oil, honey, and ground coffee. Next one introduced the provang, a thin bone rod about a yard long with a little button on the end, into *a thin bone rod* the intestinal tract by way of the rectum, and manipulated it vigorously. Thirdly, one swallowed the electuary, and concluded the treatment with a second energetic application of the provang. I feel that it was at this point in history that tea began to replace coffee as England's favored beverage.

Out of all this confusion and debate came the world's first scientific analysis of coffee. In 1685, Dr. Sylvestre Dufour described the chemical constituents of coffee with some accuracy, and apparently through numerous experiments on human beings, came to the same conclusion virtually every other researcher has come to since: Some people can drink coffee comfortably and some can't. Dufour even found a few who slept better after drinking coffee than before, probably because, in Dufour's words, the coffee "relieved their disquiet, and removed their feeling of anxiety."

Dufour also helped the critics of coffee identify for the first time their true enemy: the odorless, bitter alkaloid caffeine. The average cup of *the true enemy* American-style coffee contains about 100 milligrams of caffeine; a demitasse of espresso may contain up to twice as much. The average cup of tea contains about 70 milligrams; the average chocolate bar about 80. A 12-ounce bottle of cola contains up to 100 milligrams, about as much as a cup of coffee.

The current conclusions about the short-term psychological and physiological effects of caffeine are not so different from the first stabs in the dark by Arab physicians, or the conclusions arrived at by Dufour in the 17th century. But the long-term effects are not nearly so well understood, and are currently the subject of a vigorous, confusing, and so far inconclusive medical debate.

CAFFEINE

The short-term effects are, like the drug's history, paradoxical. The plus side is summed up by Dr. J. Murdoch Ritchie in the 1970 edition of *The Pharmacological Basis of Therapeutics:* Caffeine produces "a more rapid and clearer flow of thought," and allays "drowsiness and fatigue. After taking caffeine one is capable of a greater sustained intellectual effort and a more perfect association of ideas. There is also a keener appreciation of sensory stimuli, and ... motor activity is increased; typists, for example, work faster and with fewer errors."

a keener appreciation

Such effects are produced by caffeine equivalent to the amount contained in one to two cups of coffee. According to Dr. Ritchie the same dosage stimulates the body in a variety of other ways: the heart rate increases, the blood vessels dilate; the movement of fluid and solid wastes through the body is promoted. All this adds up to the beloved "lift."

On the minus side, we have medical descriptions of the familiar "coffee nerves." The heavy coffee drinker may suffer from chronic anxiety, a sort of "coffee-come-down," and may be restless and irritable. As we all know, he may suffer from insomnia, and even twitching muscles and diarrhea. Really large doses of caffeine, the equivalent of about 10 cups of strong coffee drunk right in a row, produce genuinely toxic effects: vomiting, fever, chills, and mental confusion. And in enormous doses caffeine is quite literally deadly. The lethal dose of caffeine in humans is estimated at about 10 grams, or the equivalent of 100 cups of coffee. One would have to drink the 100 cups in one sitting, however, which doubtless accounts for the unpopularity of caffeine as a means of taking one's own life.

simple moderation

It would seem that the answer to the coffee paradox, at least so far as short-term effects are concerned, is simple moderation. Drunk to excess coffee is quite literally a poison; drunk in moderation it is still the beloved tonic of tradition, a gentle aid to thought, labor, and conversation.

But just how much is just enough and how much is too much? Exactly where is caffeine's golden mean? No study will commit itself. I can only offer a consensus estimate based on inference. I found, for instance, no study reporting negative effects from doses of caffeine under 300 milligrams a day. Since the average cup of coffee contains about 100 milligrams of caffeine, we could *infer* from this evidence that virtually anyone should be able to drink about three cups of coffee a day and enjoy the benefits of caffeine with none of the drawbacks. Such a figure assumes, of course, that one doesn't back the coffee up with a lot of cola drinks, chocolate bars, and headache pills. This is a conservative estimate, however. One could infer from other studies that five cups a day is safe for most people. Furthermore, response varies greatly from individual to individual; some people can't drink any amount of coffee comfortably.

none of the drawbacks

So much for short-term effects. Researchers in the last 10 years or so have been busily trying to implicate coffee, particularly caffeine, in heart disease, birth defects, pancreatic cancer, and a half-dozen other less-famous

CAFFEINE

woes. So far, the evidence is contradictory and inconclusive. The clinical reports and studies continue to offer far more questions than answers, and for every report tentatively claiming a link between caffeine and some disease, several others contradict the first.

purported link

An example is the purported link between heavy caffeine intake in women during pregnancy and birth defects. In the mid-1970s, experiments indicated that the equivalent of 12 to 24 cups of coffee (or bottles of cola) per day may cause birth defects—in rats. Despite the fact that human beings metabolize caffeine differently from rats (and other researchers had questioned some of the conditions of the experiments), the United States Food and Drug Administration issued a widely publicized "warning" about the possible ill effects of caffeine on the fetus. Subsequently, an analysis by Harvard researchers of early-pregnancy coffee-drinking among 12,000 women found no significant link between coffee intake and birth defects. The upshot of the debate? The "official" position, if there is one, came from a committee of the National Academy of Sciences, which recommended what common sense, this book, and coffee lovers through the ages have always recommended: Pregnant women, according to the NAS committee, should exercise "moderation" in their intake of caffeine.

17,000 Norwegians

A similar seesaw of widely publicized negative results, countered by less-widely publicized positive or neutral results, has accompanied controversies about coffee and cystic breast disease, high blood pressure, and pancreatic and lung cancer. On the other hand, a recently reported 11-year study of nearly 17,000 Norwegian men and women found that, once the effect of smoking had been filtered out of the data, people who drank coffee actually had lower than normal rates of cancers of the colon, kidney, and skin. Norwegian researcher Erik Bjelke's report to the 13th International Cancer Congress concluded that, "while we cannot exclude the possibility that high coffee intakes may enhance carcinogenesis under special circumstances, overall, the . . . results are reassuring."

Nevertheless, anyone who drinks a regular caffeinated coffee and also is pregnant; or takes tranquilizers; or suffers from ulcers, high blood pressure or heart complaints; or is experiencing benign breast lumps (cystic breast disease); certainly ought to bring his or her coffee-drinking habits to the attention of a physician for evaluation.

In light of the continuing conflicts in the medical evidence, why are so many people so *eager* to pin blame on coffee? Partly, I think, because of the frustrations of dealing with degenerative diseases with multiple causes, like heart failure. It would be marvellous to find a simple dietary "cause" like coffee, and one that doesn't even have any food value! There is a tendency, in other words, in the face of our impotence before certain diseases, to cast about for dietary scapegoats. Coffee is ideal for such a role, not only because *a dietary scapegoat* it has no food value, but because it makes us feel good for no reason when we drink it. When we get sick I suspect we tend to fix the blame on something we already feel guilty about: coffee, wine, cake, or whatever.

The ease with which the early persecutions of coffee on religious grounds eased into condemnations on medical grounds makes the motivation behind the latest attacks on the healthfulness of coffee doubly suspect. Every culture or religion has its dietary taboos as well as its sacraments. Thou shalt not eat pork, or white bread, or meat on Fridays, or bananas on Wednesdays. A group that wishes to define its own identity must establish taboos. In the late sixties, an entire generation was busy trying to define itself as a culture distinct from the larger Western tradition. It was natural that coffee, as a social drug firmly identified with the establishment, *an establishment drug* should come under attack.

I recall, for instance, visiting an early commune where ingesting caffeine was a spiritual and dietary sin almost as bad as closing the door to undress. Yet these same puritans, so critical of caffeine, regularly reduced themselves to monosyllabic incoherence with marijuana. I recall, too, an incident at my coffee house. A customer whose age and dress indicated he was definitely not a member of the establishment told me at length why he didn't want coffee: The caffeine was bad for people. He then ordered yerba maté tea, a

pot of which contains at least as much caffeine as a mug of coffee. I told him so; he professed great interest, but still drank his maté tea. At the risk of projecting, I think his real reason for not drinking coffee was he assumed Richard Nixon, then President Nixon, drank coffee, whereas President Nixon had undoubtedly never *heard* of yerba maté tea.

These stories are not intended as criticism of the aspirations of the long-defunct counter-culture, but to point out that dietary choices, particularly of non-nutritive, mood-altering frills like coffee, are essentially irrational, arbitrary choices more akin psychologically to the fiats of religious belief or cultural prejudice than the reason of medical science. But since we live in an ostensibly rationally run, secular society, no one feels comfortable justifying his dietary prejudices on religious or cultural grounds. Instead he elevates some very tentative medical evidence into a dogma which he then defends as "scientific." Once upon a time foods were bad for the soul; now they're bad for our health. Medicine has become, in some circles, a front for religious or cultural snobbery.

mood-altering frills

a dogma

Virtually every element in our diet is currently suspect on some medical grounds or other. At a time when the average glass of drinking water is suspected of harboring carcinogens, a once country-pure herbal tea like sassafras taken off the market because it contains a proven carcinogen, and large doses of vitamin C suspected in birth defects, I see little medical reason for not drinking moderate amounts of a beverage against which nothing concrete has been proven, which has been consumed for centuries without decimating the population, and which is one of the few widely consumed modern foods which contains no multisyllabic preservatives, additives, or other adulterants.

For the ordinary coffee drinker, I think the real solution to the health dilemma is to start treating coffee with the love and attention it deserves. If one pays attention to what one's doing when one buys and makes coffee, and takes a moment to appreciate the results, many of the supposed negative effects of coffee drinking might vanish. If anyone suffers from coffee, it's

love and attention

the unconscious coffeeholic who wanders around all day with a half-filled cup of cold dishwater in his hand. I doubt whether someone who genuinely and sensually loves coffee will abuse it, any more than someone who really loves his automobile will drive recklessly.

DECAFFEINATED COFFEE

Technology to my mind is a marvelous bourgeois invention for having your cake and eating it, too. So you like coffee but not caffeine? Well then, we'll take out the caffeine and leave you your pleasure, intact. As always, technology is trying to take the bugs out of nature, and give us the garden back without the snake.

Decaffeinated coffee is indeed without venom; it contains at most one-fortieth the amount of caffeine in untreated beans, or only three percent of the original caffeine. Furthermore, the decaffeination process apparently reduces the amounts of other components of the bean which may or may not contribute to the deleterious effects coffee has on some persons.

Nor should the removal of caffeine alone alter the taste of coffee. Isolated, caffeine is a crystalline substance with no aroma and only the slightest bitter taste. As a flavoring agent it is manifestly lost in all the heady perfumes of fresh coffee. So if you hear someone say, "Coffee doesn't taste like coffee without the caffeine," he's wrong. The only real problem is how *flavor* to take out the caffeine without ruining the rest of what *does* influence coffee flavor. But technology has triumphed, more or less. The best decaffeinated coffee, fresh roasted and ground and carefully brewed, can taste so nearly the equal of a similar untreated coffee that only a tasting involving direct comparison will reveal the difference. Unfortunately, fine decaffeinated coffees are the exception rather than the norm. Decaffeinated beans are notoriously difficult to roast, and the roasting may be at fault when you buy a decaffeinated coffee that turns out to be thin bodied and tasteless. Still, anything's better than Postum, and you can always spruce up a listless caffeine-free coffee by adding a little of one of the full-bodied coffees before grinding.

Most caffeine-free coffee sold in specialty stores is shipped from the growing countries to decaffeinating plants in Switzerland and Germany, treated to remove the caffeine, then redried and shipped to the United States. The caffeine, by the way, is sold to manufacturers of medicines and soft drinks, who in turn sell their goods to people who may well have sworn off coffee.

Switzerland and Germany

Coffee is decaffeinated in its green state, before the delicate oils are developed through roasting. There are scores of patents for decaffeination processes, but those that are actually used apparently fall into one of three categories. In the oldest processes the beans were first steamed to open their pores, then soaked in an organic solvent which dissolves the caffeine. The beans are then again steamed to remove the solvent residues, dried, and roasted like any other green coffee.

This process has an obvious drawback: Minute quantities of the solvent may remain in the bean, spoiling flavor and ruining the day of any health fanatic who finds out about it. A process developed later simply soaks the green beans in hot (almost boiling) water for several hours. The water is then transferred to another tank where it is combined with a solvent which absorbs most of the caffeine. The caffeine-laden solvent is then separated from the *water*. The solvent is much easier to remove from water than from beans, because the solvent is lighter than water and never really mixes with it, whereas certain oils in the beans may actually selectively combine with the solvent, making it impossible to remove entirely.

the solvent

The water is now free of both caffeine and solvent, but still contains oils and other materials important to flavor. In order not to lose these materials, the water is returned to the first tank, where it is reabsorbed by the green beans.

The joker in the whole business is still the solvent. People who worry about the effects of coffee on their health are obviously not going to feel comfortable purchasing a product containing even minute traces of solvent (just what *does* it dissolve? brain cells; stomach tissue?). And then our

CAFFEINE

worst fears were confirmed: One of the most widely used solvents, trichlorethylene, was named a probable cause of cancer in a "Cancer Alert" issued in 1975 by the National Cancer Institute. The "Alert" was aimed at the

trichlorethylene potential health hazards trichlorethylene poses to people who work around it rather than to consumers of decaffeinated coffees, since the solvent remains in coffee in extremely minute traces. The United States Federal Food and Drug Administration, for example, permits the solvent in quantities up to 10 parts per million in ground coffee. By comparison, the doses the Cancer Institute administered to their laboratory animals were gargantuan. To match them in equivalent terms, a human being would have to drink twenty million cups of decaffeinated coffee a day for his entire life. Also, we don't know how much of the solvent residue—if any—actually makes it through the brewing process to end up in the cup. Given the volatility of the solvent and relatively miniscule amount left in the bean after roasting, I would suspect none whatsoever ends up in the coffee we ultimately consume.

Nevertheless, the notion that the caffeine we feared caused heart disease was being replaced by a solvent that actually did cause cancer threw everyone who had been virtuously drinking caffeine-free coffee for years into consternation. The coffee industry responded by replacing trichloreth-

another ylene with methylene chloride, a solvent not implicated in the National
solvent Cancer Institute's study. So far tests of methylene chloride have not implicated it in any known disease, and again, given its volatility (it vaporizes at 104°F; coffee is roasted at over 400°F for 15 minutes, then brewed at 200°F) it seems hardly possible that *any* of the one part per million occasionally found in the green beans could possibly end up in the consumer's cup or stomach.

Now the third method of decaffeination enters the picture, riding a white horse. In 1979 Coffex S.A., a Swiss firm with plants in several European countries, announced it had developed a decaffeination process using *water only*—no solvents whatsoever. Coffex will not discuss technical details, although it generously publicized the results of a tasting by coffee professionals who claim that water-only decaffeinated coffees taste fresher and better than those decaffeinated by the solvent process.

As a matter of fact, I find that coffee decaffeinated by the "Swiss water process," as it has come to be called, has *less* flavor than coffee treated by the solvent method, though possibly more body. It also costs considerably more than other decaffeinated coffees. I confess that I don't think it's worth the extra money, or the loss in flavor. Given the present sophistication of decaffeination processes, the potential solvent residue in some decaffeinated coffees is probably at most a pea under the health-conscious consumer's mattress.

"Swiss water process"

Caffeine is not the only villain in the coffee controversy. The other is certain chemicals often lumped together under the term "acid." Some people simply don't like the acid or sour note in coffee, and claim it disturbs their stomachs. Still others claim it causes jitters; there are doubtless some, particularly in California, who feel it will lead to the end of the world. I suggest that instead of taking my word for it, you experiment. Does that sourness in coffee make you feel uncomfortable in tongue or tummy? Then what you may want is not coffee with the acid taken out (such coffees do exist), but either a good dark-roasted coffee or a blended aged coffee. Dark roasting burns out most of the chemicals which cause the acid sensation, and aging mutes them. If you do your own blending, adding an old Java or aged coffee to your favorite straight coffee will produce a flavorful but very low-acid brew. There are also many coffees—some Venezuelan and Tanzanian and most Mysore, for example—that are naturally low on acid.

acid

By now you may be ready to switch to mint tea, if only you were sure it didn't cause mononucleosis in yaks. I can only urge you to treat coffee with love and respect, and hope that those who drink a lot of coffee without thinking will examine their habit, and those who worry too much about drinking moderate amounts of coffee will relax and enjoy their cup.

10 GROWING IT
How coffee is grown, processed, and graded

T O IMAGINE a coffee tree think of a camellia bush with flowers like a
jasmine. The leaves look like the camellia's: broad, dark, shiny, and
shaped like an arrow or spearhead. They are three to six inches long, and line
up in pairs on either side of a central stem. The flowers—small, white
star-shaped blossoms born in clusters at the base of the leaves—produce an
exquisite, slightly bitter scent. The flower's white color and nocturnal
aroma suggest the coffee plant prefers to be pollinated by moths or other
night-flying insects, but in fact the plant largely pollinates itself. In freshly
roasted coffee a hint of the flower fragrance seems to shimmer delicately
within the darker perfumes of the brew. The arabica plant is an evergreen; in
the wild it grows to a height of 14 to 20 feet, but when cultivated it is
usually kept pruned to about six feet to facilitate picking the beans and to
encourage heavy bearing.

the coffee tree

In some regions, Brazil for example, where there are one or two rainy
seasons each year followed by dry seasons, the hills of the plantations whiten
with blossoms all at once. In areas where there is an even rainfall all year
round, blossoms, green berries, and ripe berries all cohabit the trees simultaneously. The scent of an entire coffee plantation in bloom can be so

169

intense sailors have said the perfume reached them two or three miles out to sea. Such glory is short-lived, however; three or four days later the petals are strewn on the ground and the small coffee berries, or cherries as they are called in the trade, are forming in clusters at the base of the leaves.

small cherry

In six or seven months the berries have matured; they are oval, about the color and size of a small cherry. Within the skin and pulp are two coffee beans nestled with their flat sides together. Occasionally, as in liberated households, there are three seeds in one berry, but even more often just one, which grows small and round, and is sold in the trade as "peaberry" coffee. Each tree can produce between one and 12 pounds of coffee per year, depending on soil, climate, and other factors. The plants are propagated either from seed or cuttings. If propagated from seed a tree will take about three years to bear, and six to mature.

no extremes

Coffea arabica grows wild in the mountain rain forests of Ethiopia, where it inhabits the forest's middle tier, halfway between the ground cover and the taller trees. It will grow best wherever similar conditions prevail: no frost, but no hot extremes either; fertile, well-watered but well-drained soil (soil of volcanic origin seems best). Heavy rainfall will cause the trees to produce too much too fast and exhaust themselves; not enough rain and they will not flower or bear fruit. The trees require the same balance as regards direct sunlight: some but not too much; two hours a day seems ideal. The lacy leaves of the upper levels of the rain forest originally shaded the coffee tree; today some growers plant shade trees; others make trellis arrangements, or plant on hillsides which receive sun for only part of the day. In some mountainous areas, like the Kona coast of Hawaii, a light cloud cover forms regularly for part of the day, providing an "automatic shade."

hard bean

Whereas arabica trees planted at lower altitudes in the tropics will overbear, weaken, and fall prey to disease, trees grown at higher altitudes, around 3,000 to 6,000 feet, will usually produce coffee with a "hard bean." The slower-maturing berry produces a smaller, denser bean, less porous, containing less moisture and more flavor. We must beware, however, of easy distinctions. Some of the greatest coffees are soft bean, particularly Sumatran Mandheling and Celebes.

Coffee is sometimes grown on vast plantations, as in Brazil, where there are privately-owned *fazendas* with well over a million trees. Here processing is done on the plantation itself. Other, usually higher quality coffees, are grown on "estates," or small-to medium-sized farms. Excellent coffees are also grown by small peasant farmers in patches of a few acres at most, and processed through cooperatives. The farmer grows food crops for subsistence, and some coffee for exchange. The cooperatives, often government-sponsored, attempt to maintain and improve growing practices and grading standards.

Harvesting is one of the most important factors in how coffee tastes. Coffee berries, with the usual individualism of the brew, do not ripen uniformly. The same branch may at the same moment display ripe red berries, unripe green berries, and overripe black berries. So the conscientious grower who wants to get a high price for his coffee will pick the berries selectively; he will go over his trees again and again picking only ripe berries. Where coffee is carelessly harvested, the berries are stripped just once from the tree, ripe, unripe, and overripe all together.

harvesting

Once it is picked, coffee can be prepared either by the "dry" method, which produces what is called "natural" coffee, or by the "wet" method, which produces "washed" coffee. The "dry" method, which is the older, more primitive method, simply involves drying the berries in the sun or in a mechanical dryer, and later stripping the hard, shriveled husk off the bean, either by modern machine or with a grindstone or mortar and pestle.

dry preparation

The wet method removes most of the covering from the bean *before* it is dried. Since the moist bean is liable to damage if treated roughly, the covering must be removed gingerly, layer by layer. First the skin and pulp are gently stripped off by machine. This leaves the beans covered with a sticky, gluey substance, which if removed mechanically, would damage the

wet preparation

bean. Instead, the beans are soaked, and natural enzymes literally digest or ferment this slimy layer off the bean. This step is called "fermentation."

Next, the coffee is gently washed, and finally dried, either by the sun in open terraces, where it is continuously turned and stirred by workers, or in large mechanical driers. This leaves a last thin skin covering the bean, called the "parchment" or "pergamino." If all has gone well, the parchment will be thoroughly dry and crumbly, and as easily removed as the skin from a peanut. Some coffee is sold and shipped in its parchment cover, "en pergamino," but most often a last machine called a "huller" is used to remove it before shipping. The huller is also designed to polish the coffee, giving the flinty, dry beans a clean, glossy look especially important to specialty roasters, who sell their coffee in whole bean.

"pergamino"

The wet method is not widely used in countries like Brazil where the coffee berries ripen nearly all at once, since the labor and machinery necessary to wet process a single gigantic crop of coffee is prohibitive. In other parts of the world, Colombia for instance, there is plentiful rainfall all year round, and coffee ripens and can be processed continuously; consequently fewer workers can process more coffee, and do it better.

"Washed" coffee is not necessarily better than dry-processed or "natural" coffee. In some cases natural coffee may actually have a more distinctive flavor and more body, apparently owing to certain enzymes which remain in close contact with the bean throughout the drying process. Nevertheless, much more can go wrong with natural coffee than with washed coffee. Since drying the entire berry takes so much longer than drying washed beans, any green berries mixed with the ripe will have more opportunity to rot and impart a foul taste to the rest of the ripe berries. More importantly, most natural coffee is also strip-picked, which means there will *always* be some contamination of flavor by green or overripe berries. Most natural coffee is also dried carelessly. Processed with *care*, however, natural coffees can be as good or better than washed coffee. Most coffees carried by your specialty coffee store are washed coffees. The main exception is Arabian Mocha, and

more can go wrong

DRYING COFFEE BERRIES

GROWING IT

possibly some Ethiopian coffees, which despite primitive methods, are picked and handled with care, and are the equal of the best washed coffees.

The last step in processing is cleaning. With high-quality coffees, the beans are run on conveyor belts past workers, usually women (the wives of the men who are out moving the coffee around), who hand-pick defective beans, sticks, dirt, and other debris from the sound beans. Commercial coffees are machine-cleaned; by the time a stick or bad bean reaches you it will be ground up or freeze-dried anyhow, so only the taste buds will know.

European preparation   Coffee which has been picked over by hand is usually called "European preparation"; all specialty coffees, since they are whole bean and the consumer sees what he gets, will be European preparation.

Before marketing, coffee must be graded. Approaches differ from country to country, but there are four main criteria: how big the bean is, where (and at what altitude) it was grown, how it was prepared and picked, and how good it tastes, or cup quality. In some instances coffees are also graded by the number of "imperfections" (meaning defective and broken beans, pebbles, sticks, etc.) per kilogram. I've included more information on grading by country in Chapter 3.

GROWING YOUR OWN   The more enthusiastic among my readers may decide to begin growing their own if coffee prices keep rising; unfortunately, this is a dream few of us are in a position to realize. A true devotee of the bean would need a commercial-size greenhouse or a good-sized back yard in or near the tropics to remain well-disposed every morning the year round. First one needs a frost-free environment; this eliminates most back yards in the United States. Then figure one mature tree trimmed to about six feet should produce an average of two to four pounds of coffee a year. Including the decaffeinated coffee I consume, it would take six to eight such trees to keep me jolly. Better grow vegetables.

However, if you want just a small specimen with a few leaves to stroke in the morning and make thankful offerings to, you will have no problem.

The *Coffea arabica* is easy to grow indoors, and makes a very attractive house plant. If it likes you enough it will even reward you with flowers and berries. You can start your coffee plant three ways. The easiest is to buy a seedling. Though it's not an extremely popular house plant, most indoor nurseries carry the arabica at least occasionally. The next easiest method is to take a clipping from a friend's plant and root it. Finally, you can plant some green coffee beans, and wait . . . and wait. . . . Fresh beans sprout in about three or four weeks, but obviously the green beans that reach you through your corner coffee store will be at least a couple of months old. But if you're patient, and you plant a *lot* of beans (most won't germinate at all, ever), you might eventually have yourself a plantation.

a house plant

Beans should be planted a little over a half-inch deep, in good, well-drained potting soil, and kept moist at all times, but not wet. When you have something that looks like a plant, treat it as you would a camellia: rich, well-drained soil, always moist but never wet, with plenty of bright indirect, or diffused sunlight. Fertilize every other month. If something goes wrong, look up camellia in a good gardening manual for the appropriate advice.

If you do live in a *totally* frost-free area you might well want to plant some arabica in your yard. Temperatures should not be lower than 60° normally, and lower than 50° for short periods only. Parts of Hawaii are unsurpassed for coffee, and it has long been held that coffee could be successfully grown commercially along the California coast, but never tried because of high labor costs. Remember, however, that you need to duplicate the conditions of the Ethiopian rain forest: moist, fertile, well-drained soil and partial shade; this last would be especially important during the long summers in southern California. For more advice on growing, pruning (very important if you wish your tree to produce more coffee), and caring for coffee trees, read A. E. Haarer's *Coffee Growing* in the Oxford Tropical Handbooks series, Oxford University Press.

in your yard

11 COFFEE HOUSES
How to get it when you're out, have fun, and threaten the establishment

EVERY SOCIAL LUBRICANT has its home away from home, its church, as it were, where its effects are celebrated in public ceremonies and ritual conviviality. Alcohol has its bars, saloons, and dance halls, and opium its dens. The café or coffee house, the social home of coffee, is literally as old as the beverage itself. The first people to enjoy coffee as a beverage rather than medicine or aid to meditation apparently did so in coffee houses in Mecca in the late 15th century. The nature of the coffee house was established early, and has changed remarkably little in 500 years.

Jean de Thévenot describes a Turkish coffee house of 1664 in his *Relation d'un voyage fait au Levant:* "There are public coffee houses where the drink is prepared in very big pots for the numerous guests. At these places guests mingle without distinction of rank or creed; nor does anyone think it amiss to enter such places, where people go to pass their leisure time. In front of the coffee-houses are benches with small mats, where those sit who would rather remain in the fresh air and amuse themselves by watching the passers-by. Sometimes the coffee-house keeper engages flute-players and violin-players, and also singers, to entertain his guests."

a Turkish coffee house

COFFEE HOUSES

The "very big pots" of De Thévenot's café have become today's espresso machines or coffee urns, the "benches with small mats," outdoor terraces. And though the café shares many qualities with the bars, saloons, and *boîtes* beloved of drinkers of spirits, it has maintained its own subtly unique identity.

social gestalt

The peculiar social gestalt of the café appears to be intimately connected to the effect coffee and caffeine have on the nervous system. Coffee provokes conscious or mental associations, whereas alcohol, for instance, provokes automatic or instinctual associations. In other words, alcohol typically makes us want to eat, fight, make love, dance, and sleep, whereas coffee encourages us to think, talk, read, write, or work. We drink wine to relax, and coffee to drive home. For the Moslems, the world's first coffee

"wine of Apollo"

drinkers, coffee was the "wine of Apollo," the beverage of thought, dream, and dialectic, "the milk of thinkers and chess players." It was the faithful Moslem's answer to the other wine, the Christian and pagan wine of Dionysus and ecstasy.

Hence the customers of coffee houses from their inception in Mecca down to the present tend to talk and read rather than dance, play chess rather than gamble, and listen contemplatively to music rather than sing themselves. The café also has a greater tendency to open itself to the street and sun than bars or saloons, whose walls and darknesses protect the drinker against the encroachment of the sober, workaday world. Rather than subterranean refuge, the coffee drinker wants a comfortable corner from which to read his newspaper, observe, and pass judgement on the world as it slips by, just beyond the edge of his table.

informal study

The café is intimately connected with work (the truck stop, the coffee break), and with its own special brand of informal study and intellectual loafing. A customer with his nose buried in reading matter is a common sight in even the most low-brow cafe. The Turks called their cafés "schools of the wise." In 17th- century England coffee houses were often called "penny universities"; for the price of entry (one penny; coffee cost two, which included newspapers) one could participate in a floating seminar which might very well include the likes of Addison and Steele. As a matter of fact, aside from the Romanticists, who temporarily switched to mountaintops, it's hard to find a famous European intellectual who didn't seem to spend the better part of his days in cafés or coffee houses. The Renaissance not only gave Europe a new world view, but coffee, tea, and cocoa as well. It must have been rather difficult to consider revolutionizing Western thought after the typical medieval breakfast of beer and herring.

The ideas which have issued from the cafés of history have usually been in the direction of change rather than maintenance of the status quo. Both the French and American revolutions are said to have been nurtured in cafés *revolutions* The speech which led to the storming of the Bastille took place in the Café Foy, and Daniel Webster called the Green Dragon, a famous Boston coffee house, "the headquarters of the revolution." Since coffee does encourage thought, we may very well consider it a radical beverage, as thinking leads so inevitably to invidious comparisons between what is and what could be.

At any rate, persecutions of coffee drinking and cafés have always been tinged by politics. Once tyrants have controlled newspapers, their next goal *persecutions* is to suppress talk. Early persecutions sounded religious, but very rapidly became overtly political. The governor of Mecca repressed the very first coffee houses in 1511 because "in these places men and women meet and play violins, tambourines, . . . chess . . . and do other things contrary to our sacred law." This repression, like the rest, was short-lived. Repressions followed in Cairo, and the Grand Vizier of Constantinople ordered the coffee houses of that city closed around 1600 because he said they encouraged sedition. He let the saloons stay open, however. Caught drinking your first illegal cup of coffee, you got beaten with a stick; for the second, you got sewn in a leather bag and dumped in the Bosphorus. But even such definite measures didn't stop the coffee drinkers. Floating coffee houses developed; enterprising people walked around with pots of the brew and set up for quickies in alleys and behind buildings.

COFFEE HOUSES

In 1675 King Charles II of England published an edict closing coffee houses, the apparent pretext being an extraordinary document entitled *The Women's Petition Against Coffee, representing to public consideration the grand inconveniences accruing to their sex from the excessive use of the drying and enfeebling Liquor.* Conscientiously supporting their thesis with abundant example and plentiful detail, the authors contended that since

as unfruitful as the deserts

becoming coffee drinkers, their men had become "as unfruitful as the deserts, from whence that unhappy berry is said to be brought," and that as a consequence, "the whole race is in danger of extinction." This insinuation, as readers of Chapter 9 are already aware, was a typically below-the-belt stratagem among early-day coffee-haters. The men rose to the occasion, however, with *The Men's Answer to the Women's Petition . . . vindicating their liquor from the undeserved aspersion lately cast upon them, in their scandalous pamphlet.*

But, however interested he may have been in questions of virility, Charles' real concerns were revealed in the wording of his *Proclamation:* ". . . in such Houses . . . divers False, Malitious and Scandalous Reports are devised and spread abroad, to the Defamation of his Majestie's Government, and to the Disturbance of the Peace and Quiet of the Realm." The reaction among coffee-lovers was pronounced and immediate, and only 11 days later Charles published a second edict withdrawing his first, *An Additional Proclamation Concerning Coffee Houses,* declaring that he had decided to

Royal Compassion

allow them to stay open out of "Royal Compassion." Some observers cite this turnaround as a record for the most words eaten in the shortest time by any ruler of a major nation, unsurpassed until modern times.

The tradition of the coffee house has spread virtually worldwide. Australia is paved with Italian-style cafés, and Japan has evolved its *kisatens,* a kind of elegant reinterpretation of American 1950s-style coffee shops and coffee houses. In Great Britain the espresso-bar craze of the fifties came and went, but may be experiencing a modest comeback. Other parts of Europe and the Middle East have their own ongoing traditions. In Vienna, the home of the first European coffee houses, the café tradition is reportedly undergoing a renaissance. In the United States, the 1930s and '40s brought us the classic diner, and the '50s and '60s the vinyl-boothed coffee shop, together with the coffee house, haunt of rebels, poets, and beatniks.

In the United States of the eighties the coffee shop continues to send its carafe-bearing waitresses among vinyl-encapsuled customers, angelically ministering to the bottomless cup, while on boutique row a new kind of North American café tradition is evolving. The evolution strikes me as analogous to the Japanese adaptation of the American idea of the coffee shop in the fifties. In our case, we are evolving an idea of a café based on an Italian model that hardly exists anymore in Italy, where the stand-up espresso bar has long triumphed over more leisurely traditions. Classic fifties Italian-American cafés in urban centers, like Caffè Reggio in Manhattan and Caffè Trieste in San Francisco, have influenced the evolution of a North American café that derives its atmosphere from an immigrant's nostalgic vision of the lost and gracious cafés of pre-war Italy.

a new café tradition

The American coffee house of the fifties and sixties was always another matter; like the espresso café, it usually sported an espresso machine, but stayed open later, tended to be a little darker and a little dirtier than its counterparts, and usually offered entertainment, often with a left-leaning or counter-culture slant. Such places were often supported by radical political groups or liberal churches, in an effort to "reach the youth," or they were run and owned collectively.

a little darker

With the cultural triumph of the young urban professional, coffee houses have gone out of vogue, whereas interpretations of European-style cafés are popping up wherever picturesque old neighborhoods are turning into chic new neighborhoods. Although the principal reading material in such cafés often appears to be the menu and the leading intellectual exercise choosing dessert, I feel that where there are coffee and marble-top tables, there is hope. If the cappuccini keep improving, great ideas, revolution, and good poetry may again appear on boutique row.

12 COFFEE DRINKS
Fancy, fortified, cold, and flaming coffees

This is a chapter of recipes, limited, however, to liquid recipes. They are divided into three groups: unusual hot coffee drinks, coffee drinks fortified with spirits, and iced coffee drinks.

SOME NOTES ON INGREDIENTS

Cocoa Use an unsweetened powder, as dark and perfumy as you can get. Many of the "instant hot chocolate" mixes on the market contain sugar, and even powdered milk. Besides being overpriced they are not concentrated enough to give the powerful penetration of chocolate a good mocha or other coffee-chocolate drink demands. A really good coffee specialty store should carry such a cocoa in bulk. If not, buy Van Houten's. It is not as intense and flavorful as some bulk cocoas, but it is pure and widely available.

For drinks topped with foamed milk or whipped cream, keep unsweetened cocoa powder in a shaker next to your milk steamer or coffee pot. Garnish the white stuff with a few shakes. On foamed milk it melts and forms a delicate crust.

For mochas and other drinks calling for cocoa, add 1 heaping teaspoon of cocoa powder, 1 to 2 of brown sugar, and a little grated vanilla bean to a cup of milk; heat gently or steam while stirring. This makes an excellent hot chocolate drink, and 1/3 cup of it mixed with espresso and topped with foamed milk will make a mocha fit to make Voltaire drool in his grave.

Orange and lemon peel Most commercially grown oranges and lemons have been sprayed with insecticide; even if it's a "safe" insecticide, the skin may smell like it's been pickled in fly spray. Since the skin, not the juice or pulp, is used in coffee drinks for the sake of its intensely flavored oils, you would be wise to purchase untreated or "organic" oranges and lemons at your local natural foods store. They usually taste better, too.

Heating or steaming milk I describe the Italian or espresso method of heating milk, and the machines you do it with, in Chapter 7. Rather than heating milk from the bottom, over a flame, a tube with a nozzle on the end is stuck into the milk and live steam issues out of the nozzle, gently heating the milk without imparting a boiled or heated taste, and, if you do it right, raising a head of froth or foam on top of the milk. No coffee drink made with hot milk will taste quite right unless you steam the milk, rather than heat it on the stove.

COFFEE DRINKS

Extra- and double-strength coffee Some recipes call for a coffee made stronger than usual. For recipes calling for "extra-strength" coffee make it one-and-a-half times as strong as you would normally: 3 level tablespoons per 6-ounce cup if you follow standard practice. For double-strength make it twice as strong: 4 level tablespoons per 6-ounce cup.

UNUSUAL HOT COFFEE DRINKS

All over the world people combine large amounts of hot milk with their coffee. Fill a tall glass or small bowl with one part extra- to double-strength coffee and one part hot milk, steamed if possible. Top with a dash of cocoa powder, ground nutmeg, or grated orange peel and granulated sugar. If you make the coffee with regular or Viennese roast, it is *Kaffee Milch* (German). Made with espresso or Italian roast, it is *Caffè Latte* (Italian); with dark French roast coffee *Café au Lait* (French) or *Café con Leche* (Spanish).

Latin Americans like to make their coffee very, very strong, and heat it together with a very, very large proportion of milk. *New Orleans Coffee* is a participant in this tradition. Use a dark roast or chicory blend coffee. Brew it twice as strong as usual. Combine one part coffee with two parts hot milk (steamed if possible) in a tall glass or small bowl. What some people call *Mexican Coffee* is simply about one part very strong, dark-roast coffee combined with three parts hot milk.

Which brings us to coffees topped with whipped cream. Virtually any coffee tastes good this way. Make it a little stronger than usual, and serve it in a five- or six-ounce stemmed glass, the rather thick, substantial kind that tapers outward at the top and is used for Irish coffee and other fortified beverages. The glass will permit you to enjoy the contrast between the white cream and dark coffee. Use real whipped cream. The stuff in cans is too light; it will melt in hot coffee as fast as an early snow on a manhole cover. If you care to, you can top your coffee with partly whipped cream, Irish-coffee style: Whip the cream so it's thick but not stiff. If you sweeten your coffee, do it before you add the cream. Then slide the half-whipped cream onto the coffee so it floats on the surface; sip the coffee through the cold, thick cream.

To garnish drinks made with the lighter roasts of coffee, top the whipped cream with ground cinnamon, nutmeg, or cloves. For drinks made with the darker roasts, use cocoa powder or grated orange peel and granulated sugar. Made with a light- or moderate-roast coffee, this drink is often called *Viennese Coffee;* whipped cream also speaks other languages, as in *Espresso con Panna* (Italian: espresso coffee with whipped cream), or *Kaffee mit Schlag* (German: coffee with whipped cream).

Whipped egg whites also make an excellent topping for hot coffee. The distributors of the Cappuccin-Olà milk steamer give this recipe for *Café Belgique.* Beat 1 egg white and 1/4 teaspoon vanilla extract until stiff. Put 2 generously heaping teaspoons of this mixture in each cup, and add 1/2 cup moderate- or dark-roast coffee, brewed extra-strength, and 2 tablespoons half-and-half, heated (steamed if possible). The egg white will float to the top of the cup, stained with swirls of brown. If you have an espresso brewer, try it with espresso; decrease the amount of coffee and add some milk to the half-and-half.

My favorite combination for spiced coffee is clove and orange peel, with a little lemon peel to develop the flavor of the orange. I don't like cinnamon; it seems to go dead when combined with coffee and citrus (whereas it goes into exaltation combined with apple and wine). Nutmeg, allspice, and cardamom are also interesting with coffee, but go easy with the latter. For every cup of *Simple Spiced Coffee,* place 1 large strip orange peel, 1 small strip lemon peel and 10 whole cloves in the bottom part of a drip or filter coffee pot. Drip the coffee as usual. Sweeten to taste with brown sugar. Use regular or Viennese, rather than dark, roast coffee. A heavy-bodied coffee like Sumatran or Celebes would be best.

Coffee Grog is a pleasant winter notion; you can make the grog mix in advance, store it indefinitely in the refrigerator, and add it to freshly brewed coffee by the cup.

Grog mix:
2 tablespoons butter
1 cup brown sugar
dash salt
1/4 teaspoon each ground cloves
    and nutmeg

Cream the butter, add the other ingredients, and combine thoroughly. Store in an airtight jar in the refrigerator. When you're ready to drink some, make a heavy-bodied coffee, like a Sumatran or Celebes, extra-strength. Use a regular, not a dark roast.

To each cup:

1 to 2 teaspoons grog mix
1 large strip orange peel
1 small strip lemon peel
2 tablespoons heavy cream, heated or steamed
1/2 cup hot brewed coffee, made extra-strength

Combine the ingredients in a pre-heated mug, adding the coffee last.

FORTIFIED COFFEE DRINKS

Coffee and booze not only taste good together, they relax and invigorate in a single tasty operation. Spirits and coffee contradict yet complement one another, like hot fudge and vanilla ice cream. When you put them together you're putting together Christianity and Islam, Dionysus and Apollo, the cerebral and the instinctual. If you want something philosophical to muse over when you suck your Irish coffee through the whipped cream, try that.

The most traditional fortified drink is brandy and coffee. But almost any booze goes well with coffee, including most liqueurs and several wines. Some possibilities are: brandy, grappa, Calvados (apple brandy), Irish whiskey, Scotch whisky, light and dark rum, kümmel, anisette, Cointreau, Strega, Grand Marnier, kirsch, Tuaca, Curacao, crème de cacao, sherry, tawny port, and sweet vermouth.

Café Royale or Café Gloria is dark (French or Italian) roast coffee, served with a little sugar (about a teaspoon per glass) and a lot of brandy. Fortify it with Calvados, or apple brandy, and it becomes *Normandy Coffee.*

Irish Coffee belongs to a whole family of coffee drinks, all of which add a head of lightly whipped cream to sweetened, fortified coffee in a stemmed glass. Put a teaspoon, more or less, of sugar in the glass, fill halfway to the top with hot coffee (not a dark roast; use American or Viennese), and add an ounce or so of Irish whiskey (Scotch works too); then top with whipping cream which has been beaten until it's partly stiff, but still pours. It should be soft enough to float with an even line on the surface of the coffee, rather than bob around in lumps. If the cream tends to sink or mix with the coffee, pour it into a teaspoon held just at the surface of the coffee. Irish coffee should not be stirred; sip the hot coffee and whiskey through the cool whipped cream.

You can follow the same procedure with any of your favorite coffees and liquors; if you add brandy instead of Irish whiskey and use a darker-roast coffee it becomes *Venetian Coffee.* If you make it with crème de cacao it is *Café Cacao.* Beyond that point make up your own names.

The more complicated, large-scale drinks require advance planning (they laughed when I sat down at the chafing dish), and in some cases, rehearsal. There are two main kinds: those that use light rum as the main fortifying ingredient, and those that use brandy. The brandy drinks are usually made flaming, which is why I suggest a rehearsal, in the driveway if possible. Brandy burns with an evanescent, pure blue flame when lit. The sight of the flame at the table seldom fails to provoke after-dinner awe. Such drinks have to be concocted in the evening with the lights dim, however; in sunlight the flame becomes virtually invisible and the drama negligible.

Café Brûlot, Café Diable, and *Café Flambé* are all very similar drinks; in all cases a spiced brandy mixture is heated, lit, and combined with a strong after-dinner coffee. A richly flavored coffee is best, like a Colombian, Sumatran, or Yemen Mocha. Use a regular, rather than dark, roast. Before serving, this mixture needs to be gently heated and stirred to dissolve the sugar, and raise the temperature of the brandy. Brandy at cool room temperature won't ignite.

To each cup:

2 teaspoons sugar (try brown)
1-1/2 jiggers brandy
10 whole cloves
1 large strip orange peel
1 small strip lemon peel
1 cup hot brewed coffee, made extra-strength

Combine the sugar, brandy, cloves, and orange and lemon peels in a chafing dish. Stir gently to dissolve the

COFFEE DRINKS

sugar. Fill the glasses or cups two-thirds full of coffee, and place around the chafing dish. When the brandy has been gently warmed (you should be able to smell it very clearly from three feet away if it's ready), pass a lighted match over the chafing dish. The brandy should ignite. Let the brandy burn for as long as you get a reaction from your audience (but not over half a minute), then ladle over the coffee. The flame will usually die when the brandy is ladled into the glasses. *Don't let the brandy burn too long,* or the flame will consume all the alcohol.

If you don't have a chafing dish, put the sugar in each glass *before* you add the coffee; heat the brandy, cloves and citrus on the stove. When the fumes are rising, pour into a fancy bowl and bring to the table. Carefully lay an ounce or two of the brandy mixture atop each glass of coffee; if you pour the brandy gently it will float on the surface of the coffee. To ignite the brandy pass a match over each glass; to douse the flame mix the brandy and coffee.

If you have trouble getting the brandy to float, try holding a teaspoon right on the surface of the coffee, and pouring the brandy mixture onto the spoon, letting it spread from there over the surface of the coffee. Remember, too, to add the sugar to the *coffee,* not the brandy mixture, or the sugar will make the brandy too heavy to float. If you're serving only one or two cups, you can heat the brandy

mixture right in the ladle. Done right, this can make a smooth conclusion to an intimate dinner.

The same drink can be made with light rum. Follow the instructions I gave earlier, substituting rum for brandy, and omitting the flame business. Still another possibility is half rum and half brandy.

The best rum recipes, however, add butter and brown sugar, and are usually called coffee grog, or some other hearty nautical name. Here's a good one: Return to the recipe for coffee grog described earlier; spike it with a jigger of rum, brandy, or a mixture of both. Make sure that your coffee is hot and your mugs preheated, since the cream, spirits, and grog mix will rapidly cool lukewarm coffee.

And here is a faster, somewhat heartier *Coffee Grog.*

To each cup:

1/2 jigger each rum and brandy (or a whole jigger of either)
1 large strip orange peel
1 small strip lemon peel
10 whole cloves
dash of ground cinnamon or a bit of stick cinnamon
1/2 cup hot brewed coffee
1 to 2 teaspoons brown sugar

Rub the inside of mugs with butter. Combine the ingredients in a saucepan or chafing dish. Heat gently just short of boiling; pour into the buttered mugs, and add a jigger or so of heavy cream, or if you prefer, drink it black.

Remember too that you can add spirits to any of the drinks that come

without it; a shot of brandy is excellent in an espresso-type cappuccino, for instance; or try adding brandy, rum, or sherry to a mocha.

COFFEE LIQUEUR

Styles of coffee liqueurs differ. Before making your own I suggest you determine which style you prefer: Kahlua, for example, is heavy-bodied and based on a dark-roast coffee; others, like Tia Maria or liqueurs based on Kona coffee, use a somewhat lighter roast. If you lean towards Kahlua, use a dark-roast coffee and go a little heavier on the vanilla and (if you use it) glycerin in the recipe below; if you prefer one of the liqueurs based on a lighter roast, use a medium-roast, acidy coffee, like a Costa Rican or Colombian, and go a little lighter on the vanilla and glycerin. You might also experiment with the sugar; the touch of molasses in brown sugar will make a heavier flavored liqueur. Your liqueur will never taste quite like the best commercial products, but you may end up liking it as well or better. Store your liqueur in tightly capped bottles in the refrigerator.

1 part finely ground, dark-roast coffee
1 part brown sugar
1 part 90 to 100 proof vodka
1 inch fresh vanilla bean per cup of ground coffee

Use a filter cone or pot to make the coffee. Heat the *same* quantity of hot water as you have coffee; in other words, if you have 2 cups of ground coffee in your coffee cone prepare only 2 cups of hot water. Slit the vanilla bean and allow it to simmer in the brewing water for 15 minutes or so. Fish it out again before you pour the water over the coffee and save it.

Pour the water over the coffee slowly, to make sure you wet all the grounds. Then pour the resulting concentrated coffee through the grounds a second time. Immediately dissolve the sugar in the hot concentrate. Add the vodka and the vanilla bean, and refrigerate in a stoppered bottle for a few days. Taste; when you can barely distinguish the vanilla tint, pour into a second bottle (or some glasses) and dispose of the vanilla bean. If you're impatient, substitute vanilla extract for the bean. Add 2 or 3 drops per cup of vodka any time after you've brewed the coffee. Variations: Substitute light rum for the vodka, or add a dash of tequila to every cup of rum or vodka. If you want your liqueur to have the very heavy body of the commercial stuff, add 2 teaspoons of glycerine.

The simple addition of chocolate turns coffee liqueur into *Mocha Liqueur*. Thoroughly mix one part hot water and one part unsweetened cocoa powder. Add 1/2 tablespoon of this mixture to every cup of the finished coffee liqueur.

ICED COFFEE DRINKS

The trick to iced coffee drinks is to make the coffee extra-strength, at least one-and-one-half again as strong as usual, so when the ice melts your coffee won't taste watery. *Café Mazagran* is strong French-roast coffee poured over ice, served with club soda on the side. Sweeten and add the soda to taste. This drink was named after a fortress in Algeria where the Foreign Legionnaires supposedly invented it while torturing Bedouins and having mysteriously elliptical conversations with Sidney Greenstreet. This classic drink may well make you feel like Humphrey Bogart, particularly if you serve the soda in a syphon and the coffee in tall glasses.

Spiced Iced Coffee is an excellent idea. For each cup, put 1 large strip orange peel, 1 small strip lemon peel, and 5 whole cloves in the bottom of your drip or filter brewer. Make the coffee about half-again as strong as usual, and chill spice and citrus and all, in a closed jar. The refrigeration will make the coffee even spicier; pour over ice in tall glasses. Serve with half-and-half and brown sugar, or sweeten it first and top with whipped cream.

If you have a blender you can blend ice, coffee, and whatever else you want into a single cold creamy coffee sensation. There is no tradition behind blended coffee drinks, so everyone makes up names of his own. I'll call this one *Creamy Iced Coffee:*

1 cup chilled brewed coffee, made double-strength
2 rounded tablespoons confectioners' sugar
3 cups chopped ice

Combine the coffee, sugar, and ice, and blend until creamy. To make what I would like to call *Creamy Café au Lait*, add 1 cup half-and-half. To take your blender to the continent, use a dark-roast coffee. Another variation: Add 2 rounded teaspoons malt powder, plain or chocolate.

You can of course add ice cream as well as whipped cream to strong iced coffee. I'm sure your imagination is quite up to it (cherries? nuts?), but in case you're blocked, here is a simple suggestion from the Caffè Mediterraneum in Berkeley; they call it a *Berliner*. Fill a tall glass halfway up with chilled Viennese (or any roast) coffee. Add a big scoop of chocolate ice cream, and top with whipped cream and a dash of cocoa powder.

Finally, you can either add spirits to many of these cold drinks, or chill the hot drinks before you add the spirits. The café cacao I mentioned earlier makes an excellent cold drink. Brew the coffee in advance and chill; mix a jigger of crème de cacao and a few ounces of coffee in a stemmed glass and top with whipped cream. Dust with cocoa powder or grated orange peel and sugar: *Chilled Café Cacao*.

Or return to the recipe for creamy café au lait. Add 2 jiggers Cointreau or Grand Marnier and 1/4 teaspoon grated orange peel, then blend: *Creamy Café Cointreau*. Cold, fortified coffee drinks are easy to invent, and a good outlet for frustrated creativity, not to mention fulfilled drunkenness. Carry on.

Don't forget that all of these dessert drinks and fortified coffees can be made with decaffeinated coffee, should you wish to revel in flavor alone and go to bed early.

WORDS FOR IT
A glossary

AA Capped letters are grade indicators usually describing the size of the bean. In Peru, for example, AAA is the largest bean; in Kenya, Tanzania and New Guinea AA; in India A.

ABYSSINIAN Former name for Ethiopia, and occasionally still applied to the lesser wild or gathered coffees from that country.

ACIDY The pleasant tartness of a fine coffee. Acid is also used to describe coffee components which ostensibly produce indigestion or nervousness in some individuals, or more precisely, to describe the actual, chemically defined acids present in coffee.

AFTER-DINNER ROAST A roast of coffee, dark brown with a bittersweet tang.

AGED COFFEE Coffee held in special warehouses for long periods. Aging reduces acidity and increases body.

ALAJUELA One of the better coffees of Costa Rica.

ALTURA "Heights" in Spanish; describes Mexican coffee which has been high or mountain grown.

AMERICAN ROAST Coffee roasted to North American tastes: medium brown.

ANKOLA One of the best coffees of Sumatra.

ANTIGUA One of the best coffees of Guatemala.

ARABIAN MOCHA Straight coffee from the southwestern tip of the Arabian peninsula, present-day Yeman.

ARABICA, COFFEA ARABICA The earliest cultivated species of coffee tree, and still most widely grown.

ARMENIA One of the better coffees of Colombia.

AROMA Describes the odor of freshly brewed coffee.

ARUSHA Coffee from the slopes of Mt. Meru in Tanzania.

AUTOMATIC FILTER COFFEE MAKERS Coffee brewers which automatically heat and measure water into a filter receptacle containing the ground coffee.

BARAHONA One of the best coffees of the Dominican Republic.

BATCH ROASTER Apparatus which roasts a given quantity ("batch") of coffee at a time.

BLEND A mixture of two or more straight coffees.

BODY The sense of heaviness, richness or thickness when one tastes coffee.

BOGOTÁ One of the best coffees of Colombia.

BOURBON A botanical vaiety of *Coffea arabica* which first appeared on the island of Bourbon, now Réunion. Some of the best Mexican and Brazilian coffees, among others, are from Bourbon stock.

BOURBON SANTOS The finest Brazilian coffee.

BRAZILIAN Straight coffee from Brazil, but more specifically, a cheap, naturally processed, fair to poor arabica coffee used until recently as the basis for most American commercial blends. Coffee sold as Brazilian in most specialty stores is a higher-grade coffee, Bourbon Santos.

BROWN ROAST Coffee roasted to North American tastes: medium brown.

BUCARAMANGA An excellent but uncharacteristically low-acid coffee from Colombia.

BUGISHU Arabica coffee from the slopes of Mt. Elgon in Uganda.

CAFFEINE The chemical agent responsible for the stimulating effect of coffee and tea; an odorless, bitter alkaloid.

CARACOL See Peaberry.

CARACAS A class of coffees from Venezuela, ranging from fair to excellent in quality.

CELEBES Straight coffee from the island of Celebes, Indonesia, now Sulawesi.

CHANCHAMAYO One of the best straight coffees of Peru.

CHICORY The root of the endive, roasted and ground like coffee.

CHINA YUNNAN Straight coffee from China.

CINNAMON ROAST Coffee roasted slightly lighter than the North American norm.

CITY ROAST, FULL CITY ROAST Coffee roasted slightly darker than the North American norm.

COATEPEC, ALTURA COATEPEC Coffee from the central mountain range in south central Mexico, Veracruz State.

COBAN One of the best coffees of Guatemala.

COFFEOL, COFFEE OIL, COFFEE ESSENCE The volatile, oily substance developed in the coffee bean during roasting.

COLOMBIAN Straight coffee from Colombia.

COMMERCIAL COFFEES Pre-ground, pre-packaged (pre-brewed in the case of instant or soluble) coffees sold by brand name.

CONTINENTAL ROAST Coffee roasted dark brown, with a bittersweet tang.

CONTINUOUS ROASTER Large commercial coffee roasting apparatus which roasts coffee continuously, rather than in "batches."

COSTA RICAN Straight coffee from Costa Rica.

CÚCUTA A coffee grown in Colombia, but usually shipped through Maracaibo, Venezuela.

DARK FRENCH ROAST Coffee roasted nearly black.

DARK ROAST Coffee roasted darker than the North American norm.

DECAFFEINATED or CAFFEINE-FREE COFFEE Coffee roasted from whole beans which have had their caffeine removed in the green state.

DEMITASSE "Half-cup" in French; half-size, or 3-ounce cup.

DJIMMAH See Jimma.

DOMINICAN REPUBLIC Straight coffee from the Dominican Republic.

DRIP METHOD Brewing coffee by allowing hot water to settle down through a bed of ground coffee.

ECUADOR Straight coffee from Ecuador.

EL SALVADOR Straight coffee from El Salvador.

ESPRESSO A roast of coffee and a method of brewing.

ETHIOPIAN Straight coffee from Ethiopia; the kind generally sold in specialty stores is plantation-grown Harrar.

EUROPEAN PREPARATION A term sometimes used to describe coffee from which imperfect beans, pebbles, and other foreign matter have been removed by hand.

EUROPEAN ROAST Coffee roasted dark brown, with a bittersweet tang.

EXCELSO A grade of Colombian coffee.

EXTRA FINE Best grade of Venezuelan coffee.

FILTER METHOD Brewing coffee by any method in which water filters down through a bed of ground coffee.

FLAVOR What distinguishes the taste of a coffee once its acidity, body and aroma have been described.

FRENCH ROAST Coffee roasted dark brown, at times nearly black, with a bittersweet tang.

GOOD HARD BEAN A grade of Costa Rican coffee grown at altitudes of 3,300 to 3,900 feet.

GREEN COFFEE Unroasted coffee.

GUATEMALAN Straight coffee from Guatemala.

HAITIAN Straight coffee from Haiti.

HARD Trade term for low-quality coffee.

HARD BEAN High-grade, mountain-grown coffee from Central or South America, so called because the cool mountain temperatures produce a slowly matured, dense bean. Also grades of both Guatemalan and Costa Rican coffee.

HARRAR, HARAR, HARARI The most noted coffee of Ethiopia, grown on plantations near the ancient capital of Harrar.

HAWAIIAN Straight coffee from Hawaii. More commonly named Kona.

HEAVY ROAST Very dark-roasted coffee, with a bittersweet tang.

HEREDIA One of the better coffees of Costa Rica.

HIGH GROWN Arabica coffees grown at altitudes over 2,000 feet, usually higher. Such coffees are superior to coffees grown at lower altitudes. The term "high grown" also figures in many grade descriptions.

HIGH ROAST Coffee roasted slightly darker than the North American norm.

HUATUSCO, ALTURA HUATUSCO One of the better coffees from Veracruz State, Mexico.

INSTANT COFFEE More properly, soluble coffee. A convenience food made by rapidly dehydrating freshly brewed coffee.

ITALIAN ROAST Coffee roasted dark brown with a bittersweet tang.

JAMAICAN BLUE MOUNTAIN A fine, classically balanced coffee from the Wallensford Estate in Jamaica.

JAMAICAN HIGH MOUNTAIN Straight coffee grown in the mountains of Jamaica and exported under the market name "high mountain supreme."

JAVA Straight coffee from the island of Java, Indonesia.

JIMMA, DJIMMAH Coffee from southwestern Ethiopia, usually a naturally processed, wild coffee inferior to plantation-grown Harrar coffees.

WORDS FOR IT

JINOTEGA One of the better coffees of Nicaragua.

KALOSSI The best Celebes or Sulawesi coffee.

KENYA Straight coffee from Kenya. The best grade is AA.

KILIMANJARO Coffee from the slopes of Mt. Kilimanjaro in Tanzania.

KIVU Arabica coffee from Zaire grown near Rwanda-Burundi border.

KONA Straight coffee from the Kona (southwestern) coast of the island of Hawaii.

LIGHT FRENCH ROAST Coffee roasted slightly darker than the North American norm.

LIGHT ROAST Coffee roasted lighter than the North American norm.

LONGBERRY HARRAR Coffee grade from Ethiopia.

MAM Acronym for Medellín, Armenia, and Manizales, three of the most famous and best coffees of Colombia.

MANDHELING The most famous coffee from Sumatra.

MANIZALES One of the better coffees of Colombia.

MARACAIBO One of the best coffees of Venezuela.

MARAGOGIPE *(Mah-rah-goh-shzee-peh)* A variety of *Coffea arabica* which first appeared in Brazil, and has since been planted all over the world.

MATAGALPA One of the better coffees of Nicaragua.

MATTARI One of the best coffees of Yeman.

MBEYA Coffee from the south of Tanzania.

MEDELLÍN One of the best coffees of Colombia.

MEDIUM ROAST, MEDIUM HIGH ROAST Coffee roasted to standard North American tastes: medium brown.

MELIOR or PLUNGER-TYPE BREWER Melior is the brand name of a popular French brewer which separates spent grounds by forcing a filter down through the coffee.

MÉRIDA One of the best Venezuelan coffees; usually classed as a Maracaibo.

MEXICAN Straight coffee from Mexico.

MIDDLE EASTERN, "TURKISH" COFFEE Coffee ground to a powder, sweetened, brought to a boil and served grounds and all.

MILD A trade term for high-quality arabica coffees. Often contrasted with "hard," or inferior coffees.

MOCHA Straight coffee from the southwestern tip of the Arabian peninsula, present-day Yeman; named for the ancient port of Mocha. Also a drink combining chocolate and coffee.

MOCHA HARRAR Name for the peaberry grade of Harrar coffee from Ethiopia.

MOCHA-JAVA A blend of (usually) one part straight Arabian Mocha coffee and two parts straight Java Arabica. The world's oldest blend.

MOSHI Coffee from the slopes of Mt. Kilimanjaro in Tanzania.

MYSORE Straight coffee from Mysore, south central India.

NAIROBI Coffee from the slopes of Mt. Kenya in Kenya.

NATURALS, NATURAL-PROCESSED COFFEE Coffee processed by the "dry" method, in which the husk is removed from the bean after the coffee berries have been dried.

NEAPOLITAN MACCHINETTA A style of drip coffee brewer associated with Naples.

NEW ENGLAND ROAST Coffee roasted lighter than the North American norm.

NEW GUINEA Straight coffee from New Guinea.

NEW ORLEANS COFFEE Dark-roasted coffee blended with up to 40 percent chicory.

NICARAGUAN Straight coffee from Nicaragua.

OAXACA (Wah-*hah*-kuh) Straight coffee from the southern Mexican state of Oaxaca.

OCOA One of the better coffees of the Dominican Republic.

OPEN-POT COFFEE Coffee brewed by steeping (not boiling) ground coffee in an open pot.

ORIZABA, ALTURA ORIZABA One of the better coffees from Veracruz State, Mexico.

PARCHMENT One of the three skins of the coffee fruit, lying between the outer skin and the pulp and the innermost, or "silver" skin.

PEABERRY A small, round bean formed when only one bean develops at the heart of the coffee berry, rather than the usual two.

PERCOLATION Technically, any method of coffee brewing in which hot water percolates, or filters down through, a bed of ground coffee. More commonly refers to a coffee maker which utilizes the bubble power of boiling water to force water up a tube and over a bed of ground coffee.

PERGAMINO See Parchment.

PERUVIAN Straight coffee from Peru.

PRIMO LAVADO, PRIME WASHED A grade of Mexican coffee, which includes most of the fine coffees of Mexico.

PYROLYSIS The chemical breakdown, during roasting, of fats and carbohydrates into the delicate oils which provide all of coffee's aroma and most of its flavor.

QUAKERS Discolored or deformed coffee beans.

RANTEPAO Coffee from the island of Celebes or Sulawesi, Indonesia.

REGULAR ROAST Coffee roasted to North American tastes: medium brown.

RIOY A medicinal, iodine-like flavor in certain mass-harvested and processed coffee beans.

ROBUSTA, COFFEA ROBUSTA A botanical species of the genus *Coffea;* the only significant competitor to *Coffea arabica.* Robusta produces coffee of inferior quality, which is increasingly used as a basis for instant coffee blends.

SANANI One of the best coffees of Yemen.

SANTO DOMINGO Former name for Dominican Republic, and often still used to indicate that country's coffee.

SANTOS Coffee-growing region in southern Brazil, named after its principal port.

SHARKI One of the best coffees of Yeman.

SHORTBERRY HARRAR Coffee grade from Ethiopia.

SIDAMO Coffee from south central Ethiopia; inferior to plantation-grown Harrar coffees.

SPANISH ROAST Coffee roasted dark brown, with a bittersweet tang.

SPECIALTY COFFEE Custom whole-bean coffees sold in bulk by country of origin or roast.

STRAIGHT COFFEE An unblended coffee from a single country, region, and crop.

STRICTLY HARD BEAN The highest grade of Guatemalan and Costa Rican coffees.

STRICTLY HIGH GROWN Highest grade of El Salvador coffee.

STRICTLY HIGH GROWN WASHED Highest grade of Haitian coffee.

SULAWESI See Celebes.

SUMATRAN Straight coffee from Sumatra.

SUPREMO Finest grade of Colombian coffee.

TANZANIA Straight coffee from Tanzania, formerly Tanganyika.

TARRAZU One of the best and best-known coffees of Costa Rica.

TURKISH COFFEE See Middle Eastern coffee.

VACUUM METHOD A brewing method which differs from the filter method in that the boiling water is drawn through the ground coffee by means of a vacuum.

VENEZUELAN Straight coffee from Venezuela.

VIENNESE Describes either a coffee *roasted* slightly darker than usual, a *blend* of about two-thirds regular-roasted beans and one-third dark-roasted beans, or a coffee drink topped with whipped cream.

WASHED COFFEE Coffee prepared by the "wet" method, which involves removing the skin and pulp from the coffee bean while the berry is still moist. Most of the world's great coffees are processed by the wet method.

WHOLE BEAN Coffees which are roasted, but not yet ground.

YEMEN Straight coffee from Yemen. See Mocha.

YUNNAN Coffee from south China, near the Vietnam border.

ZIMBABWE Arabica coffee from Zimbabwe, formerly Rhodesia. Best grade is 053.

SENDING FOR IT
A list of resources

The best place to buy your coffee, and most of your brewing gear, is at your neighborhood coffee specialty store. Look in the yellow pages under "Coffee Dealers—Retail" and "Gourmet Shops." If that fails I offer the following, which is not meant as a list of my favorite specialty coffee sellers, but rather as a selection of reliable coffee roasters who offer their wares through the mail. I wouldn't have space to list all the fine shops I've visited, plus the many excellent firms which sell wholesale only, like Mountanos Brothers and United Coffee in San Francisco, and Coffee Bean International in Portland.

ORDERING COFFEE THROUGH THE MAILS

If you buy a grinder, keep your whole-bean coffees sealed, and grind a little at a time just before brewing, you can order up to about three weeks' supply at a time and always have reasonably fresh coffee. Your alternative is to buy a large quantity of green coffee, which keeps almost indefinitely, and roast your own.

Ground coffees will not keep well, however, even in the freezer, so if there is no specialty coffee store nearby and you don't buy a grinder, you might as well stash this book between your college political science text and last year's best seller and buy some canned coffee.

All of the firms I list below welcome mail orders and promise prompt service and freshly roasted coffee. Write or call for order forms and latest prices.

Seattle
Starbucks Coffee
2010 Airport Way South
Seattle, Washington 98134
Telephone: (206) 447-1575
A conscientious roaster offering 11 straight coffees and 10 blends, including decaffeinated. Phone orders accepted. Sliding shipping charges; will ship by air. Brochure available.

San Francisco Bay Area
Peet's Coffee and Tea, Inc.
P.O. Box 8604
Emeryville, California 94662
Telephone: (415) 653-7876
One of the oldest specialty coffee roasters in the San Francisco Bay Area, Peet's has survived two changes in ownership to emerge unscathed as the Bay Area's leading roaster in the European style: Peet's roasts its coffees a shade darker than most of the competition and specializes in full-bodied blends like the locally famous Major Dickason's. Peet's currently offers 16 superb straight coffees, including an aged Sulawesi; 11 blends; and six decaffeinated coffees, including exotica like a decaffeinated aged Indonesian. Two pound minimum; shipping and handling runs from $2.20 to $3.10 for a two-pound order.

Los Angeles
Polly's Gourmet Coffee
4606 East 2nd Street
Long Beach, California 90803
Telephone: (213) 433-2996
Polly's offers 26 straight coffees and 20 blends, and will custom-roast your choice of blend or straight coffee if you order five pounds or more of it. Three dollar shipping charge regardless of weight or destination.

San Diego
Pannikin
645 G Street
San Diego, California 92101
Telephone: (619) 239-1257
Pannikin sells over 16 straight coffees, seven blends and over eight caffeine-free blends, and charges a sliding scale, from $2.50 to a maximum of $5.50, for postage and handling.

New York City
Paprikas Weiss Importer
Dept. SF1
1546 Second Avenue
New York, New York 10028
Telephone: (212) 288-6117
Paprikas Weiss is a gourmet foods and cookware concern. Their catalog not only lists their coffees (eight straight coffees, seven blends, one caffeine-free blend, and one unspecified green coffee), but also hundreds of other food and kitchen items, including a small assortment of brewers, grinders, and roasters. The charge for postage, handling, and insurance is $5, regardless of weight and destination.

Zabar's
2245 Broadway
New York, New York 10024
Telephone: (212) 787-2000
Zabar's is the Metropolitan Museum of delicatessens, with bargain-basement prices. One of two authorized North American importers of the Wallensford Estate Blue Mountain coffee, Zabar's also carries several additional straight coffees, six blends, a decaffeinated dark roast, and water-only process decaffeinated. Minimum order is five pounds.

Washington, D.C.
M. E. Swing Co., Inc.
1013 E Street NW
Washington, D.C. 20004
Telephone: (202) 628-7601
A classic roaster from the pre-boutique era, Swing's offers a small but excellent selection of coffees at low prices. Their packing charge of 30 cents is more than reasonable, and they simply add UPS charges to your bill. No minimum order.

ORDERING ACCESSORIES THROUGH THE MAIL

The best place to buy the brewers and grinders and other gear recommended in these pages is at your local specialty coffee store. Large metropolitan department stores now carry a decent selection of coffee accessories, though you usually won't find the higher-end espresso machines, grinders, roasting apparatus, or other exotica. The urban-sprawl style of discount department store usually carries blade-style grinders and an assortment of the cheaper automatic-filter and filter brewers.

With the growth of specialty catalog sales to young professionals (who are too busy making money to go out and spend it), several excellent mail-order sources of coffee brewing and grinding accessories have added themselves to the old favorites. For the isolated or armchair aficionado I recommend the following:

Paprikas Weiss, Importer
Dept. SF1
1546 Second Avenue
New York, New York 10028
Telephone: (212) 288-6117
The Paprikas Weiss catalog is a flimsy, endearingly old-fashioned little item, and lists some hard-to-find, similarly old-fashioned coffee gear, like the Corona Grain Grinder and a $20 stove-top coffee roaster.

Williams-Sonoma
P.O. Box 7456
San Francisco, California 94120
Telephone: (415) 421-4242
At the other extreme from the Manhattan patchwork graphics of the Paprikas Weiss catalog, the glossy California-style Williams-Sonoma publication presents its cooking gear in slippery four-color splendor. The prices are not cheap, the selection is not old-fashioned, but the average catalog presents an impressive array of the sort of high-end accessories carried by good coffee specialty stores.

Community Coffee
P.O. Box 3778
Dept. C
Baton Rouge, Louisiana 70821
Telephone: (800) 523-8555
These small, four-color catalogs describe an excellent selection of accessories, including two versions of the old-fashioned drip pot.

William Glen
2651 El Paseo Lane
Town & Country Village
Sacramento, California 95821
Telephone: (916) 485-3000
Another glossy, California-style publication in shimmering color, the William Glen catalog offers a changing selection of classic coffee gear.

The Chef's Catalog
3215 Commercial Avenue
Northbrook, Illinois 60062
Telephone: (312) 480-9400
The Chef's Catalog carries a substantial assortment of coffee paraphernalia at reasonable prices.

Pannikin
645 "G" Street
San Diego, California 92101
Telephone: (619) 239-1257
The Pannikin brochure lists an intelligent, thorough selection of coffee gear.

Whole Earth Access
2950 Seventh Street
Berkeley, California 94710
Telephone: (800) 845-2000
In California (415) 845-3000
An Aquarian back-to-the-land empor-

ium turned yuppie discount department store, Whole Earth Access offers outstanding prices on one of the best available selections of quality coffee accessories, including a wide range of espresso brewers (not all are in the catalog, however), conventional brewers, grinders, and the Corona Grain Mill. The catalog is a substantial volume which evaluates products in detail, but costs more than catalogs ought to cost.

Zabar's
2245 Broadway
New York, New York 10024
Telephone: (212) 787-2000
The catalog graphics are casual, the mail-order selection spotty, the phone response offhand, but the prices are outstanding.

FOR THE ESPRESSO AFICIONADO

I recommend two stores that produce no catalogs, but offer some of the most knowledgeable advice available in regard to high-end home espresso machines:

Peet's Coffee and Tea
2916 Domingo Avenue
Berkeley, California 94705
Telephone: (415) 843-1434
Peet's carries many of the higher-priced home espresso machines recommended in Chapter 7.

Thomas Cara
517 Pacific Avenue
San Francisco, California 94133
Telephone: (415) 781-0383
Thomas Cara specializes in the traditional piston-style home espresso machines, and currently offers bargain prices on some rebuilt models.

Alessi stove-top espresso maker

INDEX

INDEX

BIOGRAPHICAL NOTES

KENNETH DAVIDS' vocation of writing and his avocation of coffee drinking inevitably culminated in this book. His fascination with coffee began in Europe in 1958; he admits to having spent much of his life since in coffee houses and cafés, drinking coffee, talking, and writing. Born in Chicago, Davids graduated from Northwestern University and later received his master's degree in English from the University of California at Berkeley. He has lived in Europe, Mexico, and Hawaii, his travels including several weeks spent among coffee roasters and fanciers in Great Britain preparing the British edition of this book. He eventually carried his love for cafés to the point of co-owning and managing one in Berkeley. At present he teaches and is Director of General Education at California College of Arts and Crafts in Oakland. His other published works include translations from the Hawaiian language and a novel, *The Softness on the Other Side of the Hole*, published by Grove Press in 1968.

M. L. DUNIEC was born in Germany and raised in Longview, Washington. She received a bachelor of fine arts in printmaking at California College of Arts and Crafts and has taught art at Lower Columbia College in Washington. Currently living in Edmonds, Washington, with her husband and daughter, she works as a free-lance artist and spends her free time etching and drawing.